HISTORIC GUIDE TO

ROSS BAY CEMETERY

VICTORIA B.C. CANADA

JOHN ADAMS

Sono
Nis
Press

VICTORIA B.C. CANADA

Canadian Cataloguing in Publication Data

Adams, John, 1949-
    Historic guide to Ross Bay Cemetery, Victoria, B.C., Canada

    Includes index.
    ISBN 1-55039-091-0

    1. Ross Bay Cemetery (Victoria, B.C.)—Guidebooks. 2.
Cemeteries—British Columbia—Victoria—Guidebooks. 3.
Victoria (B.C.)—Guidebooks. I. Title
FC3846.61.A33 1998   917.11'28   C98-910550-4
F1089.5.V6A33 1998

Originally published in 1983 with the assistance of
a grant from the British Columbia Heritage Trust.

We acknowledge the support of the Canada Council for the Arts
publishing program.

We acknowledge the assistance of the Province of British Columbia,
through the British Columbia Arts Council.

cover: Historic photo *circa* 1885   PABC 42413
cover design: Jim Brennan

Published by

Sono Nis Press
PO Box 160 Winlaw, BC V0G 2J0
1-800-370-5228

sononis@netidea.com
www.sononis.com

Printed in Canada by
MORRISS PRINTING COMPANY LTD.
Victoria, British Columbia

History of Ross Bay Cemetery

The Setting

The history of the property which now forms Ross Bay Cemetery is a fascinating one. To set the scene, it is useful to describe the original setting since it has changed so radically over the last 150 years. Imagine the sweeping curve of Ross Bay from Moss Street on the west to St. Charles Street on the east: high clay banks at each end of the wide bay gently sloped down toward a low flat area in the middle (at present-day Memorial Crescent) where a wide stream (the South Fairfield Stream) emptied into the Juan de Fuca Strait. During the winter, storm waves washed away parts of the low banks on either side of the stream, just as parts of the existing Dallas Road cliffs still fall away each year. Near the eastern end of the bay where the shoreline was higher, the East Creek flowed through a gully and onto the beach where it had worn a deep cleft in the clay. Between the two watercourses and along most of the shoreline, trees were stunted and sparse, forming the natural pine parklands so common to this part of early Victoria.

Inland from the beach across where the cemetery now is, the ground sloped gently upward to a broad swampy expanse that stretched from slightly north of Fairfield Road all the way to the base of the Government House escarpment at today's Richardson Street. In fact, it was this swamp which fed the East Creek and another smaller watercourse, the West Creek. The West Creek crossed under Fairfield Road just west of present-day Arnold Avenue and flowed toward the Juan de Fuca Strait, then veered westward until it joined the South Fairfield Stream on what is now Bushby Street, just west of Memorial Crescent. From there they flowed into Ross Bay as one. To the west of the cemetery, the mass of Moss Rocks rose up then, much as it does now, and the South Fairfield Stream flowed around its southern slope, draining the Fairfield Swamp which was bounded roughly by today's Moss, May, Cook and Oxford streets.

Aboriginal people had established an encampment (probably seasonal) near what is now the foot of St. Charles Street. It had been abandoned by 1850 when the Hudson's Bay Company negotiated a treaty with the Chilcowitch for lands from the sandy bay east of Clover Point (Ross Bay) to Oak Bay. But First Nations peoples continued to use the South Fairfield Stream as a means of reaching the Inner Harbour for

Ross Bay Cemetery and Neighborhood

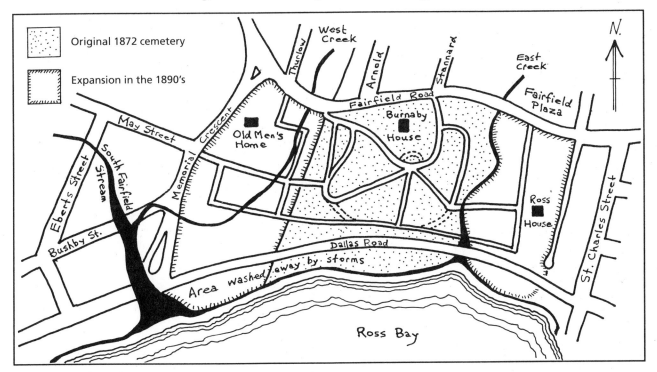

many years. This route (up the stream to the Fairfield Swamp then down another stream which flowed westward into the Inner Harbour through what are now the St. Ann's Academy grounds) was a safer route during winter storms than around Beacon Hill.

Isabella Ross and Her Farm

In 1852, James Douglas purchased all the land between Beacon Hill Park on the west to the middle of Ross Bay on the east, and from Dallas Road on the south to Fort Street on the north. He called his tract Fairfield Farm Estate. His eastern boundary line ran through the western part of what is now Ross Bay Cemetery, just behind the present caretaker's shed, and right beside the giant pine tree that marks the grave of Charlie Kincaid who was murdered by his girlfriend, Bella Adams. (See the map for Tour Five.)

In 1853, Isabella Ross purchased the land to the east of Fairfield Farm, including all the rest of present-day Ross Bay Cemetery from Charlie's pine tree and extending eastward to Gonzales Bay, including all of what is now the Chinese Cemetery at Harling Point. She called her land "Fowl Bay Farm" (the spelling that appears in the records). Unlike Douglas's property, however, Isabella Ross's extended only a short distance inland. Her northern boundary ran in a straight east-west line that today is near the back of Fairfield Plaza, cuts through the middle of Hollywood Park, runs along Lillian Avenue and continues up to the site of the Gonzales Hill weather station. Her holdings, which she purchased for £1 per acre, comprised all of section XIX (99 acres) and all of section XLVI (57 acres). It has sometimes been assumed that she inherited the property after the death in 1844 of her husband, Chief Trader Charles Ross. This has now been proven to be incorrect, so that by virtue of her purchase of section XIX, Isabella became the first woman to buy and register land in what is now British Columbia.

Isabella Ross built a farmhouse for herself and her four youngest children, who lived with her. Her oldest sons had farms of their own near Fort Nisqually, Washington Territory. The Ross farmhouse was located in the eastern portion of what is now Ross Bay Cemetery, inland from the Cross of Sacrifice, near the place where the easternmost carriageway makes a right angle turn to the west, about where the tomb of the Agnew family is located. The Ross farm produced straw and cattle, but generally it was not a venture which made Isabella wealthy.

The Ross farmhouse was on the eastern side of the East Creek. From the farmhouse to Fairfield Road, a long country lane or driveway crossed the East Creek on a small wooden bridge, then wound north-

westward up the gentle slope, joining what is now Fairfield Road (then called Foul Bay Road) at the main entrance into the cemetery, just west of Arnold Avenue. When the original portion of Ross Bay Cemetery was laid out in 1872, the old farm road formed the basis for several of the main carriageways. When the cemetery was expanded to the east in 1906, new roads were laid out directly on the drive right past the old Ross farmhouse.

From 1859 until the early 1870's, Isabella Ross subdivided all of her holdings into large parcels and sold most of them to her children. One buyer was Robert Burnaby who in 1859 purchased a strip which ran from Fairfield Farm on the west to the East Creek. Burnaby in turn subdivided a small portion and also built a house (probably for himself) in what would become the Presbyterian Section of Ross Bay Cemetery, slightly west of the carriageway opposite the end of Stannard Avenue. In 1872, 13 acres of his property (including the house) were sold to the Cemetery Trustees for $300 per acre. This piece became the first portion of Ross Bay Cemetery and, according to C. C. Pemberton who lived on nearby Moss Rocks, the few neighbors were not very happy at the prospect of having a graveyard in their midst.

It was also in the year 1872 that Isabella sold to her son Alexander the western portion of her remaining holdings, from the East Creek to present-day Wildwood Avenue. Isabella continued to live at Ross Bay with Alexander's family, but following Alexander's unexpected death in 1876 the family were in very reduced circumstances. In 1878 they were obliged to subdivide and sell all his property, including the farmhouse. Two large lots were surveyed from the East Creek to present-day St. Charles Street lane along the eastern boundary of the cemetery. After changing hands several times, these were purchased separately by the City of Victoria in 1894 and 1906 to expand the cemetery.

Isabella Ross died in 1885 while being cared for by the Sisters of St. Ann and was buried in Ross Bay Cemetery on land that had once belonged to her, within sight of her old home and facing the bay that bears her name. Just as it is often assumed mistakenly that Isabella inherited her farm from Charles Ross, many people believe that Ross Bay was named after him, too. Nevertheless, it is more likely that Isabella herself was the namesake.

Cemetery Expansion in the 1890's

In 1892, in anticipation of future expansion needs, the City of Victoria purchased a strip from the estate of the late Sir James Douglas at the western side of the cemetery. This strip comprised all the land from the

A photograph taken circa 1885 from a point near the front of the present cemetery office. Note the entrance gates in the upper left of the picture. They were located opposite Stannard Avenue. Courtesy Provincial Archives of B.C., PABC No. 42413.

western fenceline (beside Charlie Kincaid's grave) to what is now Memorial Crescent, but was then called Lover's Lane. The West Creek flowed down to the sea diagonally across this land. The parcel had been leased for many years from the Douglas family by various tenants, and a house had been built on it close to where the Rithet mausoleum is now in the north-western corner of the cemetery.

In the 1880's, the dwelling had served as an exclusive private boys' school, but after 1892 the City decided to convert it into the "Old Men's Home" for indigent men. Some people believed it was cruel to locate the elderly so close to their impending graves, but on the contrary, the men said they found that watching the frequent funerals was an interesting diversion. Eventually the house was demolished, and after 1909, the western addition to the cemetery was opened for burials.

Two of the most significant physical changes to Ross Bay Cemetery occurred in 1909 and 1911. Until this time, the cemetery extended all the way to the beach, and some graves were located only a few feet from the shoreline. Since the 1850's, Dallas Road had been laid out around the waterfront from Beacon Hill, but when it reached the South Fairfield Stream, it ended. A narrow thoroughfare, originally called Lover's Lane (now Memorial Crescent), provided access up to Fairfield Road. During the winter of 1909, storms were

particularly violent and much of the existing shore-line at Ross Bay was washed away, including a strip of the cemetery. Many graves, mostly those of Chinese and Japanese, were exposed and some disappeared completely. To prevent such events in the future, the City decided to build a concrete seawall in 1911 along the length of Ross Bay. This also provided the opportunity to extend Dallas Road. The work necessitated relocation of some graves and the grading of the bank at the eastern side of the bay. The Chinese community took advantage of the work to move as many remaining Chinese burials as possible to the new Chinese Cemetery at Harling Point.

The West Creek and the South Fairfield Stream were probably channelled through culverts soon after 1909. The route of the West Creek through the cemetery is marked by a few gratings and low-lying ground behind the caretaker's shed, but the course toward Memorial Crescent is lost. The East Creek was a more prominent landmark and was filled in gradually up until the early 1920's. A shallow depression and several gratings pinpoint its dog-leg route from Fairfield Road to Ross Bay, and on a calm day the sound of flowing water can be heard distinctly. The fire-hat tombstone of Fred Medley is within the filled-in area. For many years a vestige of the East Creek was visible near the brow of the bank overlooking Ross Bay. Here the creek had cut a deep, wide gully where it emptied into the sea. This was partially filled, and the hollow was used until the 1980's by cemetery groundskeepers for dumping leaves and burning refuse.

By World War I, it was evident that Ross Bay Cemetery one day would be too small to serve the growing population of Victoria. An offer to purchase additional land in the vicinity of what is now Hollywood Park to the east of the cemetery was given serious consideration. Instead, in 1923, Royal Oak Burial Park was created north of the city to serve both Victoria and Saanich.

The Cemetery Plan

In 1872, the Victoria Cemetery Trustees purchased 12 acres of land at Ross Bay for the new cemetery. In their plan for the cemetery, they were conforming to cemetery planning ideals popular during much of the nineteenth century.

Napoleon had decreed in 1803 that cemeteries should be separate from churches and located outside towns. The reform of cemetery layout started then and spread to Britain by the 1820's and to the United States by 1831. English horticultural planners such as John Claudius Loudon wrote treatises on cemetery design, planting and management. Typically the "new" cemeteries were to be in the countryside in a picturesque setting. A well-drained site with a southern exposure was preferred. Arrangement of plots was not left to chance but was based on a grid. Monuments, trees, flowerbeds, carriageways, chapels, fences and gates were to add to the overall effect in order to improve public morals, taste and even the intellect. The new rural, garden cemeteries in many cities in the eastern United States pre-dated formal public parks and served the purpose of providing space for quiet contemplation and strolling. Mount Auburn Cemetery in Boston had become a major tourist destination by the 1840's.

Ross Bay Cemetery incorporated many of these nineteenth century precepts. Several people probably influenced its design, but Edward Mallandaine, an architect, signed his name to the original plan. It included winding carriageways radiating from a central axis, taking advantage of the contours of the ground to provide vistas over the Strait of Juan de Fuca to the snow-capped Olympic Mountains in the distance. Formal flower beds were included in the original design, but were probably never built. For a number of years, plantings were sparse, but eventually a traditional cemetery planting plan was introduced. This included extensive use of trees and shrubs considered appropriate for cemeteries, such as holly, yew, English hawthorn, boxwood, laurel and ash. Most were

planted to flank the main carriageways. During the 1930's and 1940's the empty ground between the carriageways was planted with a wide variety of trees, especially pines, ornamental cherries and plums. At this time the Dallas Road frontage was planted with salt-resistant trees to soften the view of the cemetery from passing passenger ships.

Due to pressure from some local churches, Ross Bay Cemetery was divided into sections by religious denomination: Church of England (Anglican), Roman Catholic, Presbyterian, Wesleyan Methodist and Reformed Episcopal. An area for "heathens" (mostly Chinese Buddhists and non-Christian First Nations) was allocated in the south-western corner next to the potter's field, where the indigent were buried at public expense. Only a small section was reserved for "general" use. The Anglican, Catholic and Presbyterian churches still manage their own sections, but all other sections reverted to City-managed general use after 1879. It is noteworthy that divisions were based on religion, not necessarily race. For example, there was no section reserved for African-Americans; they were buried in the sections that accorded with their Christian affiliation.

Ross Bay Cemetery as a Place to Visit

Today's Ross Bay Cemetery shows its unmistakable nineteenth century origins. But it has evolved slowly over time to incorporate later additions, the seawall of 1911 and the plantings of the 1930's and 1940's. The layout of the additions to the cemetery after 1900 generally did not maintain the original picturesque effect, as can be seen in their straighter carriageways. In 1997 Victoria City Council designated Ross Bay Cemetery as a heritage site. This ensures that major alterations to the design in future will be reviewed by City Council before they are implemented.

Even in its expanded and mature state, Ross Bay Cemetery still embodies many of the notions that its designers in 1872 would have hoped for. It is a quiet, park-like space where many people come for a leisurely walk or for solitude. Some consider it an arboretum, one of the goals of early cemetery planners. Others marvel at its fine display of monuments, undoubtedly the largest Victorian-era assemblage in British Columbia. For them the cemetery is an outdoor sculpture garden. Lovers of history, genealogists and the plain curious can browse for hours among the tombstones. Seeing a familiar name, reading a touching epitaph or an inspirational message and contemplating the symbols of life, death and the hereafter evoke the very emotions Ross Bay's planners would have hoped for so long ago. Ross Bay, along with other cemeteries in the same style, was meant to be admired, visited and appreciated. Enjoy it as often as you can.

How to Use This Guide

In its expanded form, Ross Bay Cemetery was designed to hold about 35,000 people in double-depth plots. As of 1998 the number of burials is about 28,000. Selecting a few of the most interesting graves for a tour is always a challenge because there are so many ways to judge them. Should it include only famous people and the elaborate monuments, or is there room for others? Ease of access is also a consideration. In the final selections, a variety of people and monument styles have been included from all parts of the cemetery. Inevitably the majority of graves have been omitted, but research into all of them continues by genealogists and groups such as the Old Cemeteries Society of Victoria. The Old Cemeteries Society conducts tours at Ross Bay Cemetery or one of 20 other heritage cemeteries in Victoria each week. Over time the society manages to cover a vast number of people from all walks of life. If you are looking for information about someone buried at Ross Bay Cemetery, or have information to share, call the Old Cemeteries Society at (250) 598-8870. The e-mail address is: oldcem@cstlnet.com.

This guide is divided into 13 tours, coinciding more or less with the administrative sections imposed by the City of Victoria. Use the map at the center of the book to orient yourself to a particular section, then use the individual tour maps to plan your route. Inevitably you will find many distractions along the way to the next grave, but this is part of the enjoyment of cemetery browsing. The notes on monument makers, symbolism and monument styles at the back of the book may help you to interpret some of the monuments for yourself. The map for each section also includes notes about people buried in that section, but who have not been included in the main text. Please note that Ross Bay Cemetery has been abbreviated to RBC and Hudson's Bay Co. to H.B.Co.

Most graves are easy to find, but occasionally more detailed directions are included. Of course, things do change over time, so trees and even monuments used as landmarks may come and go. It is best to take your time and follow the tours over several visits. Sometimes it helps to have at least two people on a tour, one to read the directions and the other to locate the graves.

Funerals are less frequent in RBC nowadays, but they still take place. Etiquette suggests you avoid funeral groups or mourners at any time. Move around them and come back to that area after they have gone. Please do not let children play on the tombstones for the safety of the child and the monuments. By-laws currently limit visits to the period one hour before sunrise to one hour after sunset each day and restrict dogs in the cemetery. If you notice vandalism or anything else that troubles you while in the cemetery, please take the time to report it to one of the groundskeepers, leave a message with the City of Victoria Parks Department or telephone the police.

Walking tours of Ross Bay Cemetery have become a popular Sunday afternoon activity.
Mayor Bob Cross is seen here in 1997 leading a tour entitled "City Fathers," a tribute to Victoria's mayors who are buried at Ross Bay. The grave is that of Sen. W. J. Macdonald.

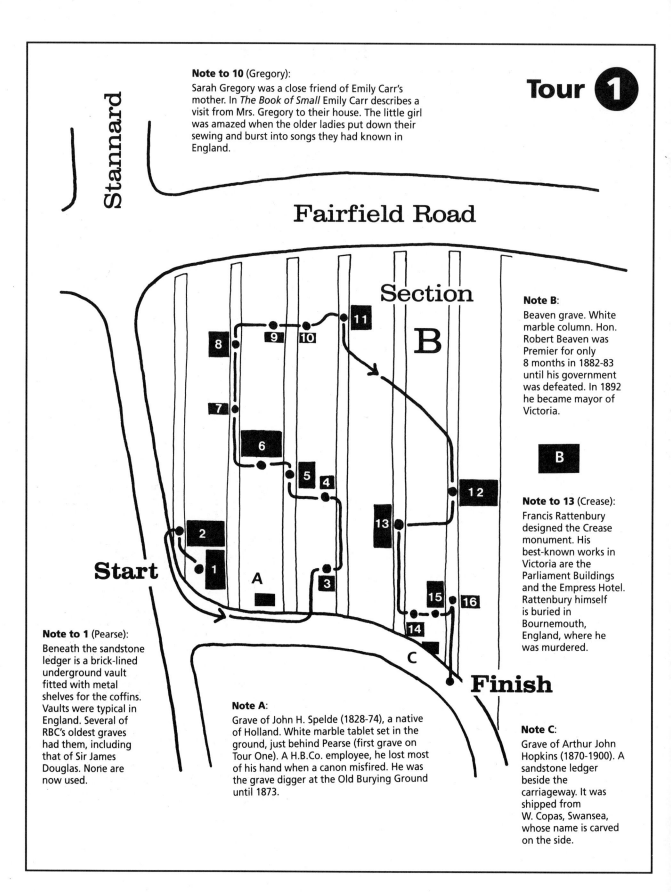

Note to 10 (Gregory):
Sarah Gregory was a close friend of Emily Carr's mother. In *The Book of Small* Emily Carr describes a visit from Mrs. Gregory to their house. The little girl was amazed when the older ladies put down their sewing and burst into songs they had known in England.

Tour 1

Stannard

Fairfield Road

Section B

Note B:
Beaven grave. White marble column. Hon. Robert Beaven was Premier for only 8 months in 1882-83 until his government was defeated. In 1892 he became mayor of Victoria.

Note to 13 (Crease):
Francis Rattenbury designed the Crease monument. His best-known works in Victoria are the Parliament Buildings and the Empress Hotel. Rattenbury himself is buried in Bournemouth, England, where he was murdered.

Start

Finish

Note to 1 (Pearse):
Beneath the sandstone ledger is a brick-lined underground vault fitted with metal shelves for the coffins. Vaults were typical in England. Several of RBC's oldest graves had them, including that of Sir James Douglas. None are now used.

Note A:
Grave of John H. Spelde (1828-74), a native of Holland. White marble tablet set in the ground, just behind Pearse (first grave on Tour One). A H.B.Co. employee, he lost most of his hand when a canon misfired. He was the grave digger at the Old Burying Ground until 1873.

Note C:
Grave of Arthur John Hopkins (1870-1900). A sandstone ledger beside the carriageway. It was shipped from W. Copas, Swansea, whose name is carved on the side.

This tour encompasses the north-western corner of Section B, one of the original parts of the 1873 layout and the one containing RBC's first interment. From 1873 to the present it has been administered by the Church of England.

1. PEARSE. A plot containing 2 white marble gabled tombstones, one with a ledger-stone in front. The marker on the south side is for Mary Laetitia Pearse (1840-72), who was the first person buried in RBC. The cemetery was being laid out at the time of her death in December 1872 and the burial predated the official opening by 3 months. Also buried in the plot is her husband, Benjamin William Pearse (1832-1902) who came to Victoria in 1851 and became Surveyor-General of Vancouver Island in 1864.

2. MACKENZIE (also McKENZIE). Mausoleum built of rough-cut gray granite blocks. Below it are the remains of Kenneth MacKenzie (1811-75) and his wife. The mausoleum itself contains the remains of other family members. MacKenzie had arrived in Victoria in 1853 to assume the duties of bailiff of the new farm, "Craigflower". The house he built, "Craigflower Manor", still stands and is operated by the provincial government as a museum.

3. WORK. White marble obelisk, by Wright & Rudge. H.B.Co. Chief Factor John Work, Sr. (1792-1861) lies at the Old Burying Ground (Pioneer Square). Here is his wife, Josette Legace, and son John Work, Jr. (1839-86). The family farm, Hillside, gave its name to Hillside Ave.

4. ASH. White marble peaked ledger-stone. John Ash, M.D. (c. 1823-86) was a former M.L.A. for Comox and a Provincial Secretary.

5. HETT. Horizontal sandstone block, with a St. Andrew's cross carved in relief across its face, in the centre of which is inscribed: JRH Ob. 1 Jan. 1880, likely for a child of J. Roland Hett (1842-91) a lawyer and the first secretary of the Victoria Cemetery Trustees.

6. TRUTCH/O'REILLY. White marble cross, draped with a wreath from which roses are falling onto the base, by Sanders of Euston Rd., London, (the only known work by this firm in RBC), marks graves of Peter O'Reilly (1828-1905) and family and commemorates his brother-in-law, Sir Joseph Trutch and Lady Trutch, both of whom are buried in Somerset, England. O'Reilly came to B.C. in 1858 and held many colonial positions. His home, Point Ellice, is now operated by the provincial government as a museum. Sir Joseph Trutch, an engineer and colonial politician, was B.C.'s first Lieutenant-Governor after Confederation (1871-76).

7. CORRIS. (Next to polished red granite round pillar). White marble tablet with clasped hands motif, laid horizontally in ground, by J. Fisher. Grave of Thomas Corris (1783-1885), who died at the phenomenal age of 102 years.

Ross Bay Cemetery's first grave, taken circa 1874. Mary Laetitia Pearse died on Christmas Day, 1872 and her burial pre-dated by three months the cemetery's official opening. Note the white picket fence which separated the cemetery from a stream and a farm to the east. The grave behind Pearse's is John Spelde's (1838-74), former grave digger at the Quadra Street Cemetery. The turned wooden posts have long since disappeared. Courtesy Provincial Archives of B.C., PABC No. 6808.

The Gothic Revival Style, one of the mainstays of Victorian architecture, found expression in Ross Bay Cemetery in this white marble tablet of 1889 for Cecilia Tyrwhitt-Drake.

Hon. John Hamilton Gray, the only Father of Confederation buried west of Ontario. Courtesy Provincial Archives of B.C., PABC No. 3086.

8. BEGBIE. Tall gray granite cross on a massive 3-tiered base. Sir Matthew Baillie Begbie (1819-94), erroneously known as the "hanging judge", came to the new Colony of B.C. in 1858 to serve as its first and only judge, often riding on horseback to far-flung gold mining centres such as Barkerville to dispense justice. The imposing tombstone actually contravenes Begbie's request that his grave be marked by "no other monument than a wooden cross . . .", although the simple epitaph bearing only his name, dates of birth and death and the words "Lord be Merciful to Me a Sinner" follows his instructions.

9. TYRWHITT-DRAKE. (Back faces No. 8). Upright, white marble, gabled Gothic tombstone, by G. Kirsop. Grave of Cecilia (1853-89), wife of William Tyrwhitt-Drake, a Victoria coal merchant.

10. GREGORY. (Under a holly tree). White marble Celtic cross with interlacing, by J. Fisher. Grave of Sarah Gregory (1838-86).

11. GRAY. Small, upright white marble cross and tablet. A plaque placed in 1981 by the Historic Sites & Monuments Board of Canada indicates that Hon. John Hamilton Gray (1814-89) was an original Father of Confederation. After 4 years as an M.P. from New Brunswick, Gray was appointed by Sir John A. MacDonald to the Supreme Court of B.C. to serve with Begbie and Crease, whose graves are located close by. (See No. 8 and 13).

12. IRVING/HAMLEY. White marble Celtic cross, around base of which is inscribed: "They too were builders of British Columbia". Buried here are Hon. Paulus Aemilius Irving (1857-1916), a Justice of the Supreme Court of B.C., and his father-in-law, Hon. Thomas Wymond Ogilvie Hamley (1818-1906), a member of the Legislative Council of the Colony of B.C. and early Collector of Customs in New Westminster and Victoria.

13. CREASE. Tall gray granite cross on a 3-tiered base. The plot is surrounded by a wrought iron fence with cast iron corner posts decorated with draped urns and torches. Marks grave of Sir Henry Pering Pellew Crease (1823-1905) and family. He became Attorney-General of Vancouver Island in 1861 and was a Judge of the Supreme Court of B.C. from 1870-1896.

14. TOLMIE. Gray granite obelisk for Dr. William Fraser Tolmie (1812-86) and family. Tolmie, a physician and botanist, went to Oregon for the H.B.Co. in 1833. He came to Victoria in 1859, and later entered politics. His son, Hon. Simon Fraser Tolmie (not buried here), was Premier of B.C. from 1928-33.

15. McNEILL. The sandstone obelisk is to Capt. William H. McNeill (1801-75) who entered the H.B.Co.'s service in 1832 and later became Master of the S.S. *Beaver*. The smaller monument is to his relict or widow, Martha (Neshaki), a Nisga'a woman. They married at Fort Simpson.

16. JESSE. White marble plaque leaning against a cross. It is in memory of George Henry Jesse, a victim of the *Valencia* disaster off Pachena Point in 1906, when 127 lives were lost.

This horse-drawn hearse was used by Hayward's to make many trips to Ross Bay Cemetery. Courtesy Provincial Archives of B.C., PABC No. 29818.

Additional map notes on Pearse, Crease, Gregory, Spelde, Beaven and Hopkins.

These sections are part of the original cemetery and have been administered by the Church of England from 1873 to the present.

1. RHODES/WALKEM. Small, white marble, truncated obelisk, with draped top. Grave of Hon. George Anthony Walkem (1834-1908), Premier from 1874-76 and 1878-82; Justice of the Supreme Court of B.C. 1882-1908. Also, of Henry Rhodes (1823-78) and family. Rhodes, Walkem's father-in-law, was a partner in Rhodes & Janion, auctioneers and merchants.

2. DE COSMOS/SMITH. Gray granite obelisk on pedestal. Graves of Amor De Cosmos (1825-1897) and Charles McKeivers Smith (1823-1911), his brother. De Cosmos, born William Alexander Smith founded the *Colonist* newspaper in 1858, was a colonial politician, Premier of B.C. (1872-74), and M.P. for Victoria (1872-82). He had become insane prior to his death and few people attended his funeral, but he has now achieved folk hero status.

3. PEMBERTON. Tall, polished red granite obelisk, by J.E. Phillips. Graves of Joseph Despard Pemberton (1821-93) and family. Pemberton had been appointed in 1851 as colonial land surveyor for the H.B.Co. on Vancouver Island and was responsible for many of the Island's earliest surveys. An elected member for Victoria in the Colonial Legislative Assembly, he owned large tracts of land in the present Fairfield and Gonzales districts.

4. PORTER. Polished red granite pedestal, with arched cornice, topped by an urn, by J.E. Phillips. Graves of the Porter brothers, Arthur (1825-1901) and James (1820-98) and families. In 1858 they established Victoria's first commercial brickyard which supplied bricks for many buildings in Old Town.

5. BRADBURY. (Behind No. 4). Polished black granite slant-faced marker with 2 bronze plaques. Thomas Bradbury (1854-1957) was a contractor and monument maker who had produced many of the tombstones in RBC. (See note on page 37);

6. FINLAYSON. Tall, polished red granite stylized Celtic cross. Graves of Roderick Finlayson (1818-92) and family. Finlayson, a clerk with the H.B.Co., had assisted with the construction of Fort Victoria and was placed in charge of it in 1844.

7. HOMFRAY. Massive, polished, dark red granite globe supported by a square-sided pedestal. The plot is surrounded by a wrought and cast iron fence and is almost engulfed by a weeping elm tree. Robert Homfray (1824-1902) was a civil engineer. A similar monument for Capt. Smallwood, by T. Bradbury, is located across the road and slightly to the south. They are the only two monuments of this style in RBC.

The massive Heathorn monument was toppled by vandals in the 1980's and one column was stolen. It has now been rebuilt and cleaned and the missing element replaced. The four arches are in the Gothic style, popular during the Victorian era. The trefoil shape of the arches symbolizes the Trinity. At the peak of the roof rests a draped urn. Urns were used in ancient Egypt and Greece for storing cremated remains and bones and were frequently used in nineteenth century cemeteries as a representation of death. Some church officials were unhappy that urns reflected the pagan custom of cremation and discouraged their use. From the number of urns at RBC alone the campaign against them apparently was unsuccessful. The drape was a Victorian affectation to soften the stark outline of the urn and to depict mourning.

Additional map notes on Hills, Fell, Houghton, Lush, Maynard and Gibbs.

Tour ②

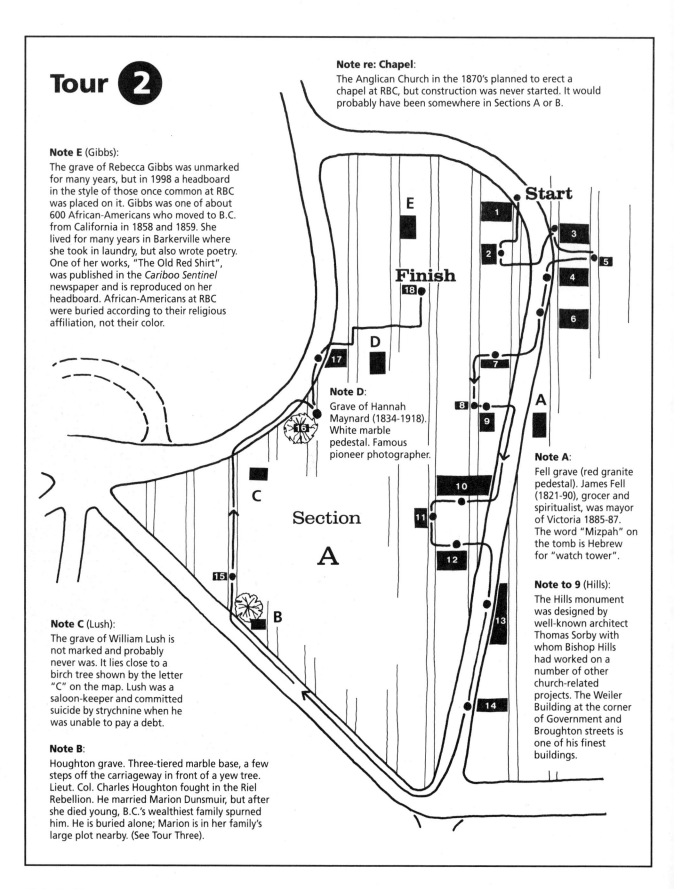

Note re: Chapel:
The Anglican Church in the 1870's planned to erect a chapel at RBC, but construction was never started. It would probably have been somewhere in Sections A or B.

Note E (Gibbs):
The grave of Rebecca Gibbs was unmarked for many years, but in 1998 a headboard in the style of those once common at RBC was placed on it. Gibbs was one of about 600 African-Americans who moved to B.C. from California in 1858 and 1859. She lived for many years in Barkerville where she took in laundry, but also wrote poetry. One of her works, "The Old Red Shirt", was published in the *Cariboo Sentinel* newspaper and is reproduced on her headboard. African-Americans at RBC were buried according to their religious affiliation, not their color.

Note D:
Grave of Hannah Maynard (1834-1918). White marble pedestal. Famous pioneer photographer.

Note A:
Fell grave (red granite pedestal). James Fell (1821-90), grocer and spiritualist, was mayor of Victoria 1885-87. The word "Mizpah" on the tomb is Hebrew for "watch tower".

Note to 9 (Hills):
The Hills monument was designed by well-known architect Thomas Sorby with whom Bishop Hills had worked on a number of other church-related projects. The Weiler Building at the corner of Government and Broughton streets is one of his finest buildings.

Note C (Lush):
The grave of William Lush is not marked and probably never was. It lies close to a birch tree shown by the letter "C" on the map. Lush was a saloon-keeper and committed suicide by strychnine when he was unable to pay a debt.

Note B:
Houghton grave. Three-tiered marble base, a few steps off the carriageway in front of a yew tree. Lieut. Col. Charles Houghton fought in the Riel Rebellion. He married Marion Dunsmuir, but after she died young, B.C.'s wealthiest family spurned him. He is buried alone; Marion is in her family's large plot nearby. (See Tour Three).

8. HEATHORN. White and gray marble monument topped by a draped urn, generally in the style of the Albert Memorial, by G. Rudge. William Heathorn (1828-90) was a tanner and manufacturer of boots and shoes.

9. HILLS. Tall, white marble Latin cross, supported by a bevelled pedestal. Grave of Maria Philadelphia Louisa Hills (1823-88), wife of the first Anglican Bishop of British Columbia. On the back of the monument is an epitaph to the Right Reverend George Hills, D.D., who died in 1895 at Parham Vicarage, Suffolk, England and was buried in the churchyard there.

10. RICHARDS. Gray granite screen supporting 2 short pilasters and a pediment. The plot is surrounded by a low boxwood hedge. Hon. Albert Norton Richards (1822-97) was Lieutenant Governor of B.C. from 1876-81.

11. DEAN. Gray granite rectangular screen bearing this epitaph: "It is a Rotten World, Artful Politicians are its bane. It's saving grace is the artlessness of the young and the wonders of the sky." John Dean (1850-1943) had lived in a log cabin on the top of Mt. Newton and had donated land there that became John Dean Park. He contested the Victoria mayoralty in 1928 and 1929 and was bitter about his defeat, thus the inscription. He had the tombstone erected in 1936 while he was still alive, his date of death remaining blank until 1943.

12. DUPONT. Tall, gray granite obelisk with etched palm leaf on front, by Cullett & Sons, Toronto. Graves of Margaret Dupont (1819-1903) and Major Charles Dupont (1837-1923) who lived at "Stadacona" on Stadacona Avenue.

13. TODD. A large plot containing several monuments, the largest being a massive, polished dark red granite Celtic cross on a heavy pedestal. Jacob Hunter Todd (1827-99) had founded the fish canning firm of J.H. Todd & Sons Ltd.

14. PRIOR. White marble variation of a Celtic cross with flowers cascading down the front. Grave of Lieut. Col. Hon. Edward Gawler Prior (1853-1920), Premier of B.C. from 1902-03.

15. MONTOBIO. (Just past the first yew tree). Upright, white marble tablet with deep relief carving of a weeping willow. Grave of G.B. Montobio (1828-89), a native of Pieve di Soli, Italy, who died in Nanaimo. He was a general merchant in Victoria.

16. WHITE. (Search for this tombstone in a large yew tree beside the roadway, just south of No. 17.) Upright, white marble tablet with a unique motif of an angel's head and wings, by G. Kirsop. Grave of Eden White (1846-84), a former proprietor of the Oriental Restaurant, Yates St.

17. WOOD. White marble statue of a mourning girl (not an angel) leaning against an urn and holding a wreath, supported by a 4-sided pedestal. George Kirsop, probably the most accomplished of the marble carvers in Victoria, was the sculptor. His signature is to the right of the footstone. Graves of the Wood family, including John Wood (1838-89), a real estate owner.

18. KEMP. Upright, wide, gray marble shouldered tablet with deeply carved inset motif of an angel holding a cross. Grave of William Gladstone Kemp (1861-77) who "met his death by accident March 8th, 1877 on board H.B.C. Barque Princess Royal at Burrard Inlet."

The weeping willow was a common tombstone motif in the nineteenth century, symbolizing mourning. Ironically, few were planted in cemeteries because their moisture-loving habits might suggest the ground was wet, an unpleasant thought to those burying the dead. The deep relief of this carving is similar to that by M. Gilardi on the Bossi tomb, Tour Six.

Tour ③

Note G:
Rogers grave. Red granite column, toward Fairfield Rd. from grave 15 (Bohrer). The Rogers family founded Rogers Chocolates. Note later addition of name of Leah Rogers (1864-1952), philanthropist, whose name was not inscribed when she died.

Note A:
Giacomo Bossi grave. Pedestal with a standing angel. Bossi was from Lombardy. He owned the Grand Pacific Hotel, Johnson at Store streets. (See his brother Carlo's grave on Tour Six.)

Note C:
The farmhouse built by Robert Burnaby was situated about here when the cemetery site was purchased from him in 1872. It was either demolished or moved to house the cemetery caretaker, near the present caretaker's shed.

Note B:
A gravel pit operated by the City of Victoria was located about here in the Presbyterian Section until the 1920's. Note the depression in the ground where it was filled in.

Finish

Section H

Note E:
Spring grave. White marble pedestal. Russian-born William Spring (1831-84), owned trading and sealing schooners. He and his wife, Susan Ciamia (1841-1909), a Sto:lo woman, were married at Yale. They had seven children.

Start

Note F:
The focal point of the original 1872 cemetery design was a semi-circular driveway. It was seldom used and was divided into plots and sold in 1981. Note the differences in styles between the recent monuments and the older ones around them.

Note D:
Ash trees line the main carriageway that borders Section H. To the Greeks they symbolized stability. In Scandinavian folklore ash trees were a symbol of immortality. In the fall, put ash keys (seeds) in your pocket to ward off evil.

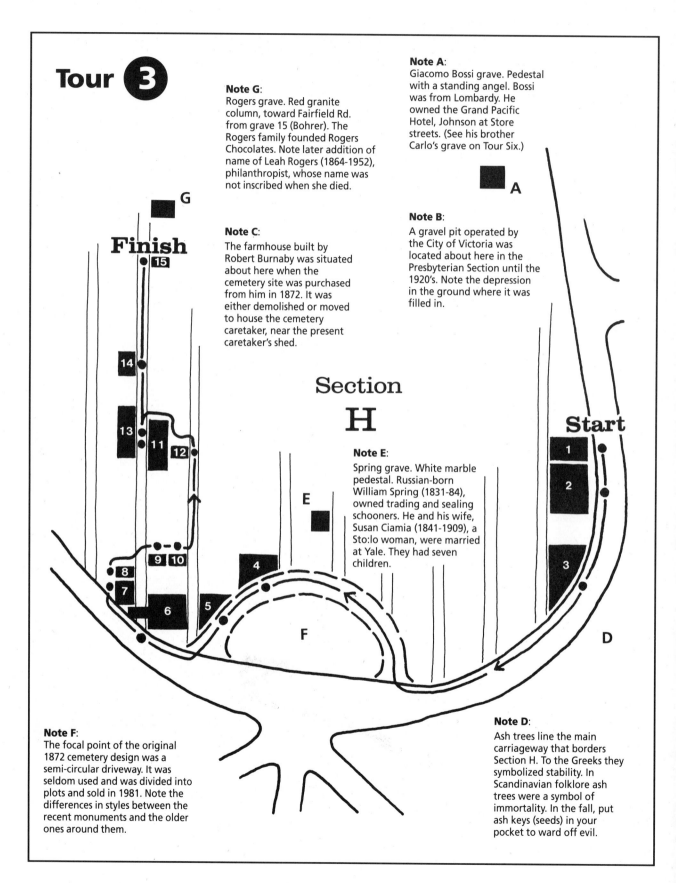

Since 1873 Section H has been administered by the Presbyterian Church, although some notable non-Presbyterians are buried in it (e.g., Douglas and Helmcken).

1. BARNARD. Polished red granite obelisk with etched floral scrollwork, by the Canadian Granite Co., Ottawa. Graves of Francis Jones Barnard (1829-89) and family. Barnard came to B.C. in 1859 and founded the renowned Barnard's Express (BX) to the Cariboo goldfields. As a colonial politician he supported Confederation and was later an M.P. for Yale-Kootenay from 1879-87. His son, Hon. Sir Frank Stillman Barnard (1856-1936) was Lieutenant-Governor of B.C. from 1914-19.

2. DUNSMUIR. Massive, polished gray granite pedestal with cornice and pediment, topped by a draped urn. The plot is surrounded by a gray granite curb. Grave of Hon. Robert Dunsmuir (1825-89) and family. He had discovered coal near Nanaimo in 1869 and at his death, when he was having Craigdarroch Castle built, was the richest man in B.C. His son, Hon. James Dunsmuir (1851-1920) was Premier 1900-02 and Lieutenant-Governor 1906-09. Note epitaph on back to James Jr. (1894-1915) who died on the *Lusitania*.

3. ROBSON/HUNTER. Polished gray granite pedestal with cornice, topped by a draped urn. Hon. John Robson (1824-1892), while Premier of British Columbia, died in London, England from blood poisoning contracted after having closed a cab door on his finger. His body was returned to Victoria and interred on July 29, 1892. In New Westminister in 1861, he founded the *British Columbian* newspaper, which he used to attack Governor Douglas. He was Premier from 1889 until his death. Also buried in the plot is his son-in-law, Joseph Hunter (1842-1935), the last surviving member of the first Legislature after Confederation (1871).

4. NESBITT. White marble obelisk with carved inset cross and shamrocks, by Wright and Rudge. For Samuel Nesbitt (1829-81) and family. Nesbitt was a Victoria biscuit and cracker manufacturer. His grandson, James Knight Nesbitt (1908-1981) "Newspaperman Historian" is buried here. Note that the curbstones of this and other nearby plots are angled because they once abutted a semi-circular driveway, a major feature of the original cemetery design which was grassed over and divided into plots in 1981.

5. DICKSON. Tall, polished red granite column topped by an urn. Note maker's inscription: J. Daniel, Pine Street, San Francisco. Graves of Susan Surrilda (1847-74) and John Dickson (1828-75), a tinsmith.

The funeral of Hon. John Robson in St. Andrew's Presbyterian Church, July 29, 1892. Courtesy Provincial Archives of B.C., PABC No. 17689.

6. DOUGLAS. Massive, polished red granite pedestal topped by a stylized Celtic cross. Plot is surrounded by a wrought and cast iron fence. A vault is located under part of the plot. Contains graves of Sir James (1803-77) and Lady (1812-90) Douglas and family. Undoubtedly one of RBC's most famous occupants, Douglas was a Chief Factor of the H.B.Co., founding Fort Victoria in 1843. He was the 2nd Governor of Vancouver Island (1852-64) and the 1st Governor of B.C. (1858-64).

7. MOSS. Sandstone, truncated obelisk with IOOF (Odd Fellows) symbols, carved by G. Kirsop. The cast iron fence includes harps, oak leaves (symbolizing strength) and acorns, with draped lamps (everlasting life) on the corner posts. Charles Moss (1821-77) was a moulder at the Albion Iron Works where the fence was likely made. The plot surface is tiled in a black and white checkerboard pattern. The IOOF symbol of heart and hand reminds us that our work should be prompted by love, not greed.

8. BAILLIE. Small, white marble obelisk. Dr. Thomas Baillie drowned off Cape Flattery in the wreck of the *Florencia* in 1860 and his body was never recovered. The monument was erected years later by his daughter when her brother died. T. B. Baillie is believed to have been the uncle of Sir Matthew Baillie Begbie. He had lived in South America and California before coming to Victoria.

9. HARPER. (Back faces No. 8). Upright, white marble tablet with inset winged cherub motif by Foster. Grave of Annie Harper who died at Seabeck W[ashington] T[erritory], May 31, 1876 aged 29 years.

Additional map notes on Bossi, the gravel pit, Burnaby's farmhouse, ash trees, Spring, the semi-circular driveway and Rogers.

10. McLEESE. (Back faces No. 9). Upright sandstone gabled Gothic tablet with motif of a broken-stemmed rose, by G. Kirsop. Graves of Mary S. McLaren McLeese who died on April 4th, 1876 and her infant daughter, Ann, 2 days before.

11. DEANS. White marble statue symbolizing faith holding her scroll and anchor, George Kirsop, sculptor. Inverted torches on the 4 corners of the pedestal represent extinguished life. George and James Deans came to Craigflower Farm in 1853. George and Annie later bought their own farm near where Camosun College's Landsdowne Campus is today. James was a poet and anthropologist.

12. JACK. Upright white marble tablet with anchor motif in relief, appropriate for James Jack (1831-82), wharfinger for the H.B.Co.

13. PEMBERTON. Unpolished light gray granite tablet. Graves of Augustus Frederick Pemberton (1807-91) and family. Once the Commissioner of Police for Vancouver Island he had lived for many years on Fairfield Road.

14. TEAGUE. Gray granite curb and footstone enclosing a grassed plot. Graves of John Teague (1833-1902) and family. Teague was one of Victoria's foremost architects, having designed City Hall in 1878.

15. BOHRER. Upright white marble tablet (with cross broken off). Note epitaph: "Such as Found Musical Tunes" (Ecclus. XLIV, 4). Professor Heinrich Bohrer (1822-82) was described by the *Colonist* as "a musical genius (who) lived only for his art". He dropped dead while giving a music lesson to one of the Misses Dunsmuir.

The remains of George Deans, farmer at Oakvale Farm, formerly of Craigflower Farm, lie beneath this classically inspired white marble pedestal and statue.

The massive polished red granite tombstone of Sir James Douglas, first Governor of the Colony of British Columbia.

1. MUNRO. Massive, polished black granite pilaster supporting a heavy cornice and pediment, topped by a casket and torch. Graves of Alexander Munro (1824-1911) and family. He was a Chief Factor of the H.B.Co. from 1874-1890.

2. RUSSELL. Upright white marble tablet with the *agnus dei* by Foster. Grave of Robert Henry Russell, (died September 7, 1869) aged 4 years, 5 months, and of his sister. Thomas Russell, their father, was teacher at Craigflower Schoolhouse in 1865. Robert Henry had died of diphtheria and had been buried in the Quadra Street Cemetery, but was exhumed when his sister died and was re-interred with her in RBC.

3. ELLIOTT. Tall, polished red granite column, topped by an urn. Grave of Andrew Charles Elliott (1829-89), Premier from 1876-78, who is described by Martin Robin as "an able lawyer and administrator but a bungling politician . . ."

4. WALKER. White bronze obelisk. Records deaths in 1890 of Mary Jones Walker (aged 24) and her infant daughter, Martha, 10 days later.

5. IRVING. Gray granite slab set in ground marks the plot of Captain John Irving (1854-1936) and family. Irving was well-known from Oregon to the Yukon as a steamboat captain and owner of the Canadian Pacific Navigation Co., the forerunner of the C.P.R.'s Coast Steamship Service.

6. CARR. A large, grass-covered plot with 2 markers: a small plaque set in the ground commemorating Emily Carr (1871-1945), "Artist and author, lover of nature"; and a polished black granite slab set on a slight slant, commemorating the other members of the Carr family interred here. This latter marker was placed in 1981 by the Emily Carr Arts Center Society.

7. HELMCKEN. A plot for Dr. James Douglas Helmcken (1858-1919) and family, and containing 5 markers. J.D. Helmcken was a son of pioneer doctor J.S.

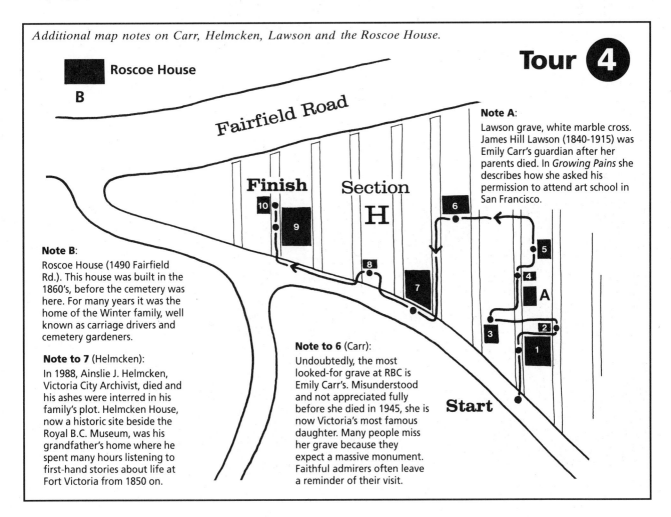

Additional map notes on Carr, Helmcken, Lawson and the Roscoe House.

Tour ❹

Roscoe House

B

Fairfield Road

Finish

Section H

Note A:
Lawson grave, white marble cross. James Hill Lawson (1840-1915) was Emily Carr's guardian after her parents died. In *Growing Pains* she describes how she asked his permission to attend art school in San Francisco.

10 **9**

6

5

8

4

A

7

3

2

1

Start

Note B:
Roscoe House (1490 Fairfield Rd.). This house was built in the 1860's, before the cemetery was here. For many years it was the home of the Winter family, well known as carriage drivers and cemetery gardeners.

Note to 7 (Helmcken):
In 1988, Ainslie J. Helmcken, Victoria City Archivist, died and his ashes were interred in his family's plot. Helmcken House, now a historic site beside the Royal B.C. Museum, was where his grandfather's home where he spent many hours listening to first-hand stories about life at Fort Victoria from 1850 on.

Note to 6 (Carr):
Undoubtedly, the most looked-for grave at RBC is Emily Carr's. Misunderstood and not appreciated fully before she died in 1945, she is now Victoria's most famous daughter. Many people miss her grave because they expect a massive monument. Faithful admirers often leave a reminder of their visit.

Helmcken. The largest tombstone in the plot is a polished red granite pedestal with an urn by G. Rudge, for Captain T. Fletcher. Its size is ironic because Helmcken had allowed Fletcher to be buried here due to the latter's presumed impoverished circumstances.

8. WALTHER. White marble pedestal topped by an urn. The plot is surrounded by a cast iron fence decorated with fleur-de-lis. Grave of Henry Walther (1843-86) of Germany, proprietor of the Bavaria Brewery. Note German epitaph which translates in English: "His life was but a moment/His dream of spring his happiness on earth".

9. HORTON/BOYD. Tall white marble column in composite Classical styles topped by a wreathed urn. This has the finest Classical detailing of any monument in RBC. Graves of John Boyd (died April 10, 1890) and others. Boyd was a dealer in groceries and liquors.

10. STEWART. Cement-covered plot with 2 polished black granite horizontal markers. The northernmost commemorates Alexander Stewart (1864-1943) and family. A. Stewart was a well-known monument maker in Victoria. (See note on page 38).

A finely carved white marble column in composite Classical styles, circa 1889, for the Boyd and Horton families.

A general view looking from the Presbyterian section to the Anglican section. In the left foreground is the monument to the Robson/Hunter family (see Tour Three). The statue in the background is on the Wood family plot (see Tour Two).

Most of Section M was part of the original 1873 Cemetery and has always been for general use. The westernmost strip was added in the 1890's.

1. RUDGE. Plot surrounded by a sandstone curb featuring carved acanthus leaves, with the name RUDGE carved in relief on the footstone, and the words "gone home" to the left and "it is well" to the right. Graves of George Rudge (1854-1934) and family, well-known in the monument-making trade. (See note on page 44.)

2. TAYLOR. White marble tablet laid flat in a cement grave cover. Grave of John George Taylor (1824-1891), a Victoria City Police detective. Note epitaph: "Erected by the managers in grateful memory of his loving benefactions to the Protestant Orphans Home" and the passage: "Charge those who are rich in this world that they may be rich in good works". (1st Timothy VI, 17-18). Taylor had bequeathed $30,000.00 to the Home's building fund.

3. HAYWARD. Polished, red granite pedestal with arched cornice, topped by an urn. Graves of Hayward family. Charles Hayward (1838-1919), Mayor of Victoria from 1900-02 was a pioneer undertaker in the city whose firm handled many of the burials in RBC. Note epitaph: "They serve God well who serve his creatures".

4. ROBERTSON. Polished, red granite twin columns supported by a screen, and topped by an urn. William Archibald Robertson (1832-1926) had fought for the North in the American Civil War and had been captured at Harper's Ferry by Stonewall Jackson, before arriving in Victoria in the mid 1860's. Here he was a prospector, carriage maker, blacksmith, alderman, school trustee, and M.L.A. Also buried in the plot are his wife who died from cancer after suffering for 6 years and his daughter who drowned in the Point Ellice Bridge disaster, 1896.

5. STARRATT. (Proceed west across paved pathway). Upright gray marble tablet with a carved anchor and star motif. Ralph Starratt (1870-93) was likely a visiting sailor. Note epitaph: "Remember friends as you pass by/ As you are now, so once was I/ As I am now you soon shall be/ Then prepare for death and follow me". It was erected by his shipmates. This epitaph was fairly common on Victorian era tombstones, and at least one other variation occurs in RBC.

6. JAPANESE. (In an open grassed area, under a large spreading pine tree). Small, white marble 5-sided plaque set flat in ground. Epitaph is in Japanese, accompanied by a succinct statement in English: "Japanese, died December 19, 1896, aged 26". The RBC *Plot Book* gives the deceased's name as Totaugh. A similar tombstone is located in Section K.

7. THOMPSON. Small, white marble shaft. Grave of Capt. Magnus Thompson, who perished from exposure at Carmanah after the wreck of the *Janet Cowan*, New Year's Eve, 1895. The unmarked graves of several other victims lie nearby. After 10 days, 22 survivors were rescued, but the bodies of the dead were only recovered four months later.

8. SMITH. White and gray marble pedestal, topped by a draped urn. Note the incised motifs of a cannon, and the Odd Fellows all-seeing-eye and linked chain. Epitaphs to: Henry E. Smith (1872-98) of the 5th Regiment, Garrison Artillery; and George Edward Smith (1830-1925) "a veteran of the Crimea"; and others.

Additional map notes on Fawcett, the caretaker's house, cremation plots, Howard, Kincaid and Totaugh.

One of the pleasures of Ross Bay Cemetery is its diversity. This photograph captures the ragged look of the Palmer grave (see Tour Six) in the spring after the daffodils have finished blooming. It appears sandwiched between two sandstone obelisks of the 1870's.

Tour ⑤

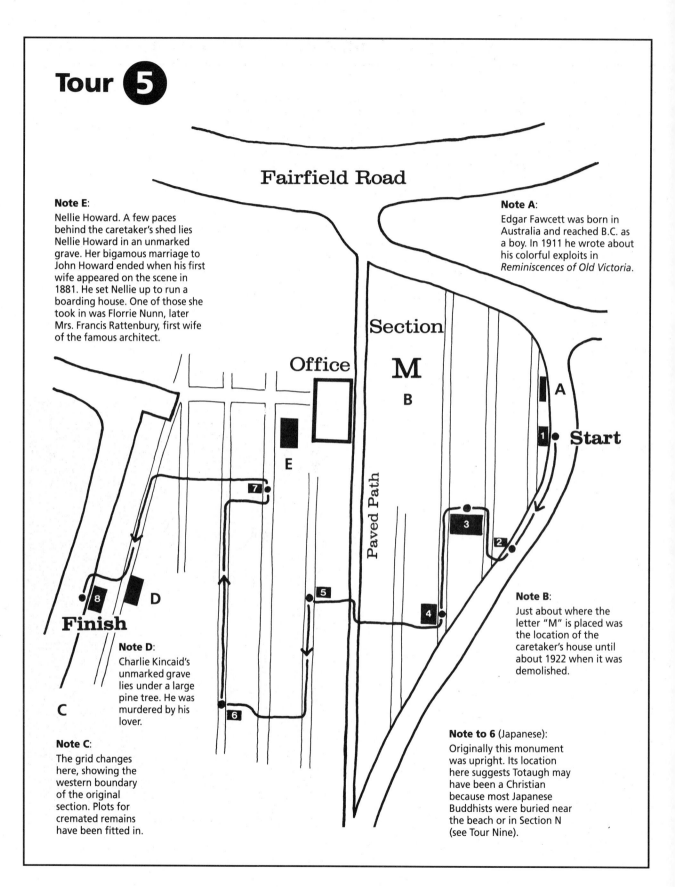

Fairfield Road

Note E:
Nellie Howard. A few paces behind the caretaker's shed lies Nellie Howard in an unmarked grave. Her bigamous marriage to John Howard ended when his first wife appeared on the scene in 1881. He set Nellie up to run a boarding house. One of those she took in was Florrie Nunn, later Mrs. Francis Rattenbury, first wife of the famous architect.

Note A:
Edgar Fawcett was born in Australia and reached B.C. as a boy. In 1911 he wrote about his colorful exploits in *Reminiscences of Old Victoria*.

Office

Section M

B

E

A

1 ● **Start**

3

2

7

5

4

8 ● **Finish**

D

C

6

Note D:
Charlie Kincaid's unmarked grave lies under a large pine tree. He was murdered by his lover.

Note C:
The grid changes here, showing the western boundary of the original section. Plots for cremated remains have been fitted in.

Paved Path

Note B:
Just about where the letter "M" is placed was the location of the caretaker's house until about 1922 when it was demolished.

Note to 6 (Japanese):
Originally this monument was upright. Its location here suggests Totaugh may have been a Christian because most Japanese Buddhists were buried near the beach or in Section N (see Tour Nine).

Section F in the original cemetery plan of 1873 was reserved for general use, but was allocated to the Reformed Episcopal Church sometime after it was started in Victoria in 1874. After 1879 it reverted to the City of Victoria. The western portion seems always to have been retained by the City and in it there is a high proportion of unmarked graves containing paupers, unknown people, stillborn babies, convicts, and native Indians.

1. BOSSI. White marble screen with Corinthian-inspired pilasters at the sides, surmounted by a draped urn, and featuring 2 relief medallions of Mr. and Mrs. Carlo Bossi. Carlo Bossi (1827-96), a native of Lombardy, Italy, had learned the marble-cutting trade there, and when he came to Victoria in 1858 one of his first jobs was hewing the pillars that graced the front of the Bank of British North America (now demolished). He later became successful in real estate and in the grocery business on Yates Street. Bossi was a prominent member of the Pioneer Society and its badge is carved between the two medallions. Petronella Bossi designed the tombstone and asked M. Gilardi, a stonecutter from Carlo's home town, to make it. Soon afterward Petronella married Lorenzo Quagliotti. Both are buried in the vault below, but Petronella's name was never carved beside Carlo's.

2. MITCHELL. Upright sandstone pilaster, surmounted by a cornice, by G. Kirsop. Features relief carving of an anchor surrounded by an oak leaf and acorn wreath, above a shield bearing the epitaph and a small St. Andrew's cross at the base. William Mitchell (1802-76) was born in Scotland and came to the Pacific coast in 1836 where he became a ship's master for the H.B.Co., sailing on the *Vancouver, Cadboro, Recovery, Una,* and *Beaver.*

3. ROSS. A large, cement-covered plot with several granite markers. Alexander Ross (1835-76) was a son of Charles and Isabella Ross. He was raised in his mother's farmhouse at the eastern end of RBC and bought it from her. When he died unexpectedly at age 41, his family was forced to sell the house. See photograph on next page of the previous Ross headboard removed in 1984 by the family.

4. and 5. LANGLEY. Matched pair of upright, white marble, shouldered tablets. Graves of Alfred John Langley (1820-96) of Langley and Co., druggists, and his wife, Mary (1837-76).

6. FARDON. White marble gabled tablet, by G. Rudge, laid horizontally in the ground. Motif of a finger pointing to Heaven. Grave of George R. Fardon (1807-86), an agent for Langley and Co.

7. CRIDGE. Massive, upright rough-hewn gray granite stone, with inset granite plaque bearing epitaph. Edward Cridge (1817-1913) came as Chaplain to the H.B.Co. at Fort Victoria in 1855, becoming Dean of Christ Church Cathedral (Anglican) in 1865. A theological dispute with Bishop Hills caused him to join the Reformed Episcopal Church in 1874, of which he was elected a bishop in 1875. The congregation built the Church of Our Lord on land donated by Sir James Douglas.

8. KEITHLEY. Gray marble triangular plaque set on a slant into a rusticated gray granite base. In memory of George Edward Keithley (1858-1912), an engineer at Taylor Mill. The triangular shape plus the incised motifs of a skull and crossbones, spears, a leaf, axes, single swords, and a sword with an open book indicate Keithley's Masonic affiliation.

9. KATAYAMA. Upright, gray marble gabled square shaft, with incised anchor motif (and a globe missing from the top), by T. Bradbury. Grave of George Katayama (1850-93). Note Japanese epitaph.

In 1897 M. Gilardi carved this white marble monument designed by Mrs. Carlo Bossi in honor of her late husband.

Tour 6

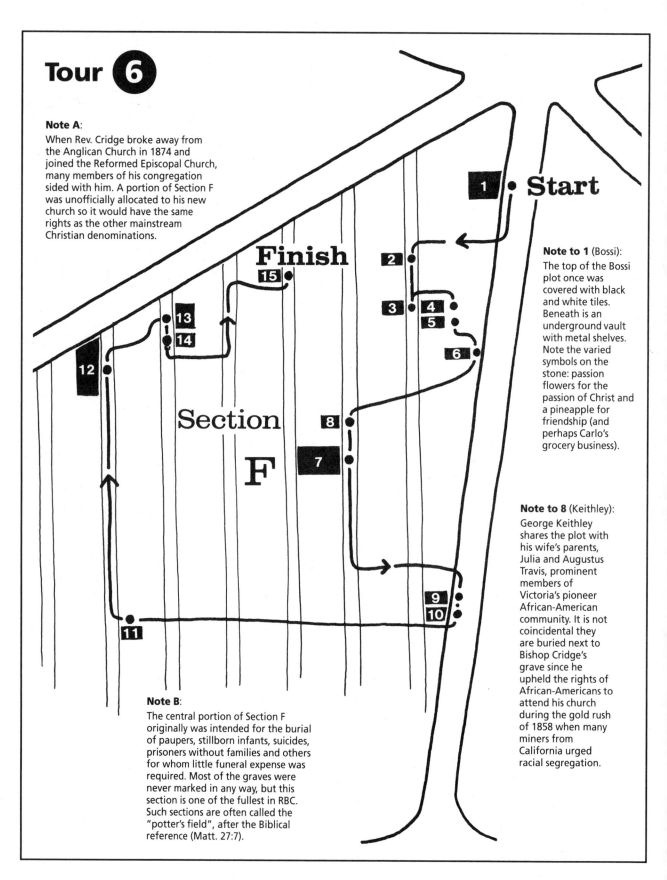

Note A:
When Rev. Cridge broke away from the Anglican Church in 1874 and joined the Reformed Episcopal Church, many members of his congregation sided with him. A portion of Section F was unofficially allocated to his new church so it would have the same rights as the other mainstream Christian denominations.

Start

Finish

Section F

Note to 1 (Bossi):
The top of the Bossi plot once was covered with black and white tiles. Beneath is an underground vault with metal shelves. Note the varied symbols on the stone: passion flowers for the passion of Christ and a pineapple for friendship (and perhaps Carlo's grocery business).

Note to 8 (Keithley):
George Keithley shares the plot with his wife's parents, Julia and Augustus Travis, prominent members of Victoria's pioneer African-American community. It is not coincidental they are buried next to Bishop Cridge's grave since he upheld the rights of African-Americans to attend his church during the gold rush of 1858 when many miners from California urged racial segregation.

Note B:
The central portion of Section F originally was intended for the burial of paupers, stillborn infants, suicides, prisoners without families and others for whom little funeral expense was required. Most of the graves were never marked in any way, but this section is one of the fullest in RBC. Such sections are often called the "potter's field", after the Biblical reference (Matt. 27:7).

10. NAGANO. Upright, gray marble shaft, topped by a globe, by A. Stewart. Grave of Tsuya Nagano, wife of Manzo Nagano, B.C.'s first Japanese immigrant (1877). Buried with her is her infant daughter. The Naganos, a Christian family from Kyushu, operated a store on Government Street.

11. BARKER. Bronze plaque set flat in the ground. (It is difficult to find but walk due west from No. 9 and it is on the edge of the open, grassed area.) Grave of Billy Barker (1819-94) whose discovery of gold in the Cariboo in 1862 started the boom town of Barkerville, now a provincial historic site. He died in poverty at the Old Men's Home beside RBC and was buried in an unmarked grave until 1962. Recent research proves he was born in Cambridgeshire, not Cornwall as once thought.

12. HARRIS/WILSON. Brown sandstone truncated obelisk with carved coat of arms and sprig of laurel, by G. Kirsop. (Originally, it may have been topped by a globe). Thomas Harris (1817-84), a butcher and proprietor of the Queen's Market, was Victoria's first Mayor (1862-65) and noted for his large size. William Wilson (1843-1920), Harris' son-in-law, was in the drygoods business.

13. PALMER. Upright, white marble tablet with inscriptions on both sides. On the western face is the Odd Fellows linked chain insignia, marking the epitaph of

The anchor symbolizes Captain William Mitchell's many years of service aboard coastal ships for the Hudson's Bay Company; the oak-leaf and acorn garland symbolizes strength; and, the St. Andrew's cross bears witness to Mitchell's Scottish birth.

This weathered headboard stood on the grave of Alexander Ross until 1984 when descendants replaced it with a granite tablet. It was the last of hundreds of wooden grave markers, crosses, fences and gates at RBC. Grass fires, the weather and vandalism took their toll on all of them one by one. It is now in storage and in 1994 was used as the pattern for the headboard of Isabella Ross, Alexander's mother. (See Tour Twelve.)

Digby Palmer (1799-1887) from Sheffield, England, who came to Victoria in 1862. He was known as Professor Palmer and gave music lessons in his Fort Street home, where his wife also gave dancing classes. A tragedy is recorded on the east face of the marker: "To the memory of Fanny aged 17 years and 7 months, a beloved daughter of Digby and Jane Palmer of Victoria, B.C., who was drowned at sea near Cape Flattery in the wreck of the steamer Pacific Nov. 4th, 1875. The body was found on the beach at San Juan Island and interred here by sorrowing friends Nov. 28th, 1875. Pray for those at Sea". Fanny was *en route* to visit her sisters in San Francisco and had had a premonition she would not return, according to newspaper accounts.

14. DYER. White marble tablet laid flat in the ground. For George Dyer (died February 13th, 1880). "Erected by his Comrades".

15. NICHOLSON. Sandstone obelisk standing on a 4-sided pedestal into which white marble plaques have been inset on each side. Graves of Thomas Nicholson (1797-1875), a teacher, and family. This style of monument was more prevalent in Pioneer Square than in RBC.

Additional map notes on Bossi, Keithley, Cridge and the potter's field.

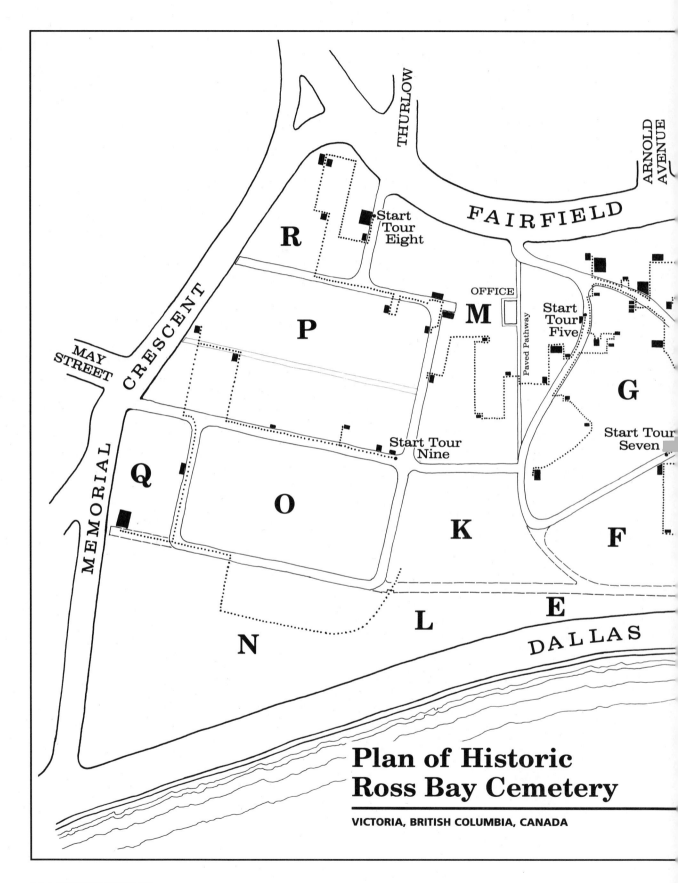

THURLOW

ARNOLD AVENUE

FAIRFIELD

R

Start
Tour
Eight

OFFICE

M

Paved Pathway

Start
Tour
Five

G

P

MAY
STREET

CRESCENT

Start Tour
Nine

Start Tour
Seven

MEMORIAL

Q

O

K

F

N

L

E

DALLAS

Plan of Historic
Ross Bay Cemetery

VICTORIA, BRITISH COLUMBIA, CANADA

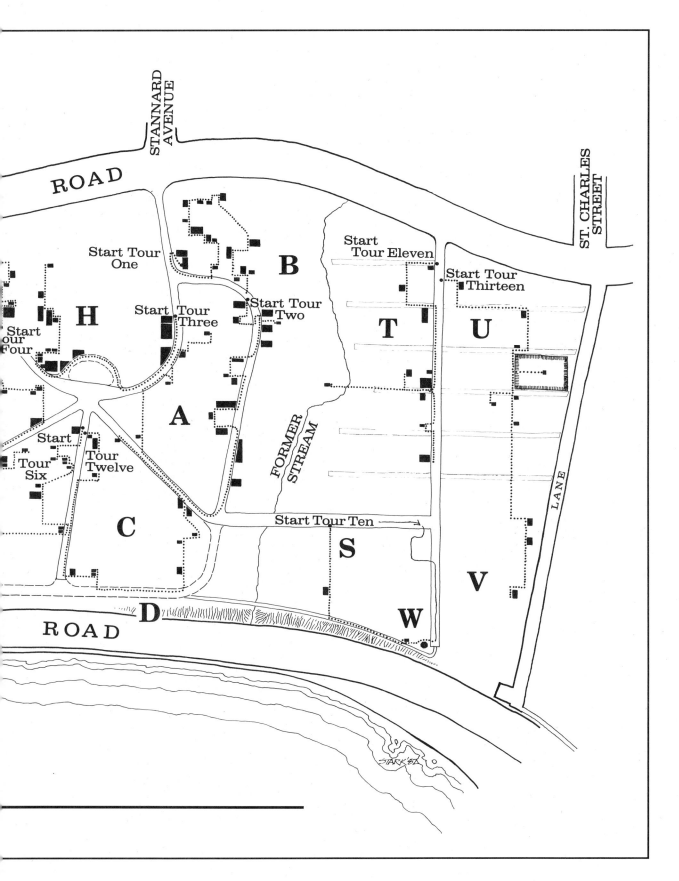

STANNARD AVENUE

ROAD

ST. CHARLES STREET

Start Tour One

B

Start Tour Eleven

Start Tour Thirteen

H

Start Tour Three

Start Tour Two

T

U

Start our Four

A

FORMER STREAM

Start

Tour Six

Tour Twelve

C

Start Tour Ten

S

W

V

LANE

D

ROAD

STARK'S

Section G was one of the original parts of RBC, and was administered by the Wesleyan Methodist Church from 1873-1879.

1. GREEN. Plot contains 2 markers: a massive polished red granite pedestal to Alexander Alfred Green (1834-91) of the banking firm of Garesche and Green, and family; and a separate mini-plot with a white marble headstone by G. Rudge, a curb, and a white marble foot plate inscribed "Baby".

2. HIGGINS. Gray granite obelisk topped by a stylized urn. Grave of D. W. Higgins (1834-1917) and others. Higgins had been an editor of the *Colonist*, an author of local histories and Speaker of the Legislature.

3. GUILD. Sandstone obelisk with inset, carved Odd Fellows symbols, by G. Kirsop. Commemorates Albert Henry Guild (1814-73) and his wife. His epitaph reads: "Past grand master, a founder of the order on this island. A true Odd Fellow. Sterling in his character and one whom our order always esteemed".

4. BOWDEN. Upright, sandstone Gothic tablet with relief carving of a dove descending from above carrying an olive branch in its mouth, by Foster. Grave of Thomas Mills Bowden (1848-74), a dentist and native of Bowmanville, C[anada] W[est].

5. CARPENTER. Small, cast "white bronze" draped obelisk, bearing the name of the White Bronze Co., St. Thomas, Ontario. Many other white bronze monuments in RBC likely were made by this firm, but this is the only one which visibly bears the manufacturer's name. Marks grave of Annie Carpenter (died July 5th, 1888).

6. WILLIAMS. Four attached, smooth white marble columns in the Tuscan style, with Corinthian capitals, supporting a draped urn and a torch, standing on a 4-sided pedestal. Marks graves of John William Williams (1829-87) and family. Williams operated a livery stable at the corner of Government and Johnson Streets. He was a Victoria alderman (1875-79) and an M.L.A. (1878-82). He died in San Bernardino, California, but his remains were brought to Victoria for burial.

7. and 8. KIRSOP. Two matching white marble tablets laid flat in the ground. The southernmost marks the grave of Ann Elizabeth Kirsop (1829-81). The northernmost marks the grave of George Kirsop (1825-8❡), one of the most prolific monument makers whose works are in RBC. (See note on page 38). Both tombstones have the same motif, an ivy-covered cross, and show considerable restraint considering the sculpting talent of Kirsop.

9. PETTIBEAU. Upright, white marble tablet with rose motif, by G. Kirsop. Grave of Anne C.V. Pettibeau (1810-80) of Paris, France. She ran a girls boarding and day school on Fort Street. Note inscription: "Erected in loving remembrance by her affectionate pupils and

The broken column was used in many Victorian era cemeteries to symbolize sorrow, but this elaborately festooned example on the grave of Leila Engelhardt is the only extant example of it in Ross Bay Cemetery.

friends". The City of Victoria received a bill for $2.50 from Mme. Pettibeau's undertaker because the City's gravedigger on the day of burial had at first refused to allow a grave case to be installed requiring an extra trip to RBC for Hayward's delivery man once special orders had been received from civic officials overruling the gravedigger.

10. FIELD. White marble tablet laid in the ground with a flying angel motif, by G. Rudge. (Look for this tombstone behind a tall yew tree). Grave of Margaret Field (1854-86), wife of Edwin Field, a salesman at David Spencer's store.

11. ENGELHARDT. (Near the Chislett Mausoleum). The plot is dominated by a polished red granite column, but look for the small white marble monument at the

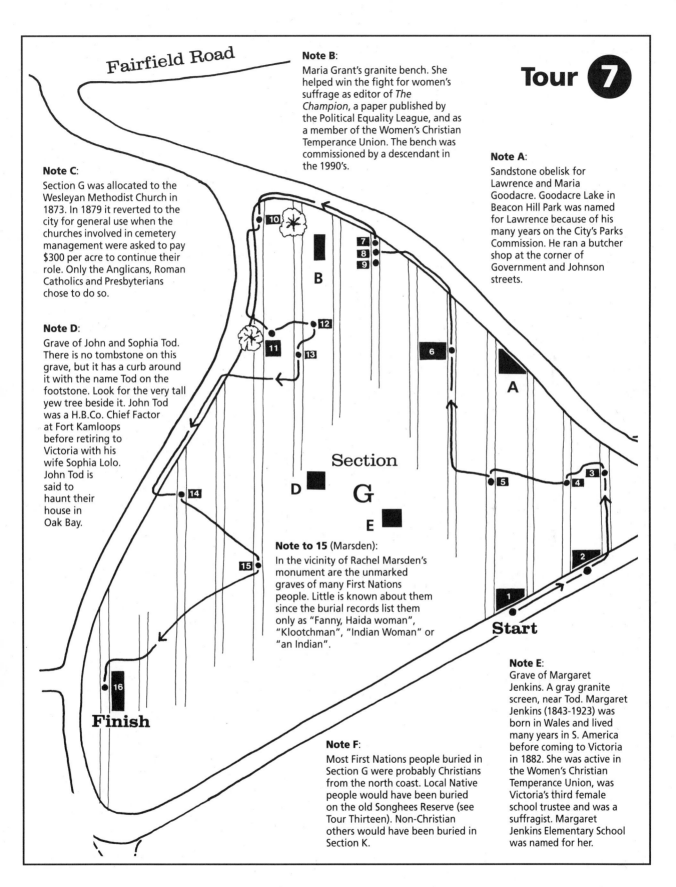

Tour **7**

Fairfield Road

Note B:
Maria Grant's granite bench. She helped win the fight for women's suffrage as editor of *The Champion*, a paper published by the Political Equality League, and as a member of the Women's Christian Temperance Union. The bench was commissioned by a descendant in the 1990's.

Note A:
Sandstone obelisk for Lawrence and Maria Goodacre. Goodacre Lake in Beacon Hill Park was named for Lawrence because of his many years on the City's Parks Commission. He ran a butcher shop at the corner of Government and Johnson streets.

Note C:
Section G was allocated to the Wesleyan Methodist Church in 1873. In 1879 it reverted to the city for general use when the churches involved in cemetery management were asked to pay $300 per acre to continue their role. Only the Anglicans, Roman Catholics and Presbyterians chose to do so.

Note D:
Grave of John and Sophia Tod. There is no tombstone on this grave, but it has a curb around it with the name Tod on the footstone. Look for the very tall yew tree beside it. John Tod was a H.B.Co. Chief Factor at Fort Kamloops before retiring to Victoria with his wife Sophia Lolo. John Tod is said to haunt their house in Oak Bay.

Section
D **G**
E

Note to 15 (Marsden):
In the vicinity of Rachel Marsden's monument are the unmarked graves of many First Nations people. Little is known about them since the burial records list them only as "Fanny, Haida woman", "Klootchman", "Indian Woman" or "an Indian".

Start

Finish

Note E:
Grave of Margaret Jenkins. A gray granite screen, near Tod. Margaret Jenkins (1843-1923) was born in Wales and lived many years in S. America before coming to Victoria in 1882. She was active in the Women's Christian Temperance Union, was Victoria's third female school trustee and was a suffragist. Margaret Jenkins Elementary School was named for her.

Note F:
Most First Nations people buried in Section G were probably Christians from the north coast. Local Native people would have been buried on the old Songhees Reserve (see Tour Thirteen). Non-Christian others would have been buried in Section K.

northern end. It is a broken column almost obscured by carved drapes and garlands, by M. Gilardi. Grave of Leila J.E. Engelhardt (died November 7th, 1884, aged 9), daughter of J. Engelhardt, a coal and wood dealer. This is the best example in RBC of the broken column motif and one of only two known monuments signed by M. Gilardi.

12. BONE. Tall, polished red granite obelisk. Note maker: Carrara Marble Works, Plymouth England. Grave of Jane Bone (died May 24th, 1881) and her husband, Thomas (1818-1897), a native of Saltash, Cornwall, which may help explain why the monument was ordered from Plymouth.

13. CARNE. Gray granite obelisk, by A. Henderson. The only known example of this Nanaimo monument maker's work in RBC. (See note on page 37.) Graves of Frederick Carne (1829-1904) and family. He had been proprietor of the Angel Hotel on Langley Street.

14. BEDNALL. Clean, white marble tablet laid flat in the ground with inset poppy motif. (A quick way to find this one is to proceed south on the roadway and look for the Astrico monument on the west side. No. 14 is almost opposite it on the east side of the road, under a *cedrus libani* tree). Grave of Eliza Bednall (1819-84). The tree's protection has preserved this tombstone remarkably well.

15. MARSDEN. White marble tablet with incised eagle and salmon motif, by Moses Venn of Metlakahtla. (To find this one from No. 14 walk towards a lone, stunted pine tree to the southeast. No. 15 is beneath the tree). This unique, crudely-worked tombstone marks the grave of Rachel Marsden (1835-70). It was produced at Metlakahtla, the Methodist native Indian model community near Prince Rupert.

16. ADAMS/HEATHERBELL. White marble column topped by an urn, by A. Stewart. The pedestal base contains epitaphs of 4 people, all of whom drowned, 3 in the Point Ellice Bridge disaster, May 26th, 1896, and one, Frederick Adams (1842-95), a contractor for the Parliament Buildings, who went down with the tug *Velos* on March 22nd, 1895 while it was *en route* to Haddington Island to pick up limestone.

Additional map notes on Goodacre, Grant, the section's management, Tod, Jenkins, First Nations' graves and Marsden.

The dove descending from Heaven is a symbol of the Holy Spirit.

These imposing white marble columns on the grave of John William Williams combine the smooth shafts of the Tuscan style with acanthus leaves on the capitals.

The western boundary of the original 1873 cemetery corresponds with the western boundary of Section M. In 1893 the City of Victoria bought what are now Sections R and P, once part of Sir James Douglas' estate. Until 1904 the civic "Old Men's Home" was located in Section R, an unfortunate juxtaposition which daily reminded the residents of their impending final earthly destination. Section P had its first burial in 1900; Section R in 1904.

1. RITHET. Gray granite mausoleum in Romanesque style. Contains loculi for coffins of Robert Patterson Rithet (1844-1919) and family. Rithet was Mayor of Victoria in 1885, and an M.L.A. from 1894-98. He operated the mercantile house of R.P. Rithet and Co., and was responsible for the construction of the Outer Wharves.

2. HARRIS. Gray granite pilaster laid on a slant. Graves of Dennis R. Harris (1851-1932), a C.P.R. survey official, and Martha Douglas Harris (1854-1933), youngest daughter of Sir James Douglas. They were married in 1878.

3. PENDRAY. Upright, polished black granite tablet. Grave of William Joseph Pendray (1845-1913), a Victoria soap manufacturer whose plant was located at Laurel Point. His Queen Anne style house on Belleville Street has been restored for use as a restaurant.

4. BREWSTER. Upright, polished black granite pilaster with a cornice etched with a "B". Grave of Harlan Carey Brewster (1870-1918), Premier of B.C. from 1916 until his death.

5. PHILLIPS. Polished, red granite screen supporting a horizontal cylinder, and bearing Masonic insignia. Joseph Eva Phillips (1850-1908) made many of the tombstones in RBC. (See note on page 38).

6. CHUNGRANES. Five upright tombstones in a row. Note the middle 3 made of white marble are deeply sculpted with motifs of flying doves, flowers, and a cherub. No maker's name appears. Graves of family of Demetrius K. Chungranes (1857-1919) of Greece, a dealer in fish, meat and vegetables.

7. ROSS. Polished gray granite screen topped by pilasters supporting a pediment. Graves of Dixi Harrison Ross (1842-99), a grocer on Government Street, and his wife. (No relation to Ross of Ross Bay.)

8. GRANT. Tall, polished red granite obelisk, by J. E. Phillips. Note epitaph to William Grant (1877-98) who "died on Skagway Trail". (See note on map.)

9. ANSCOMB. Double sepulchral sarcophagi, consisting of gray granite pillars supporting a pediment, by Stewart Monumental Works. Two polished red granite plaques enclose the ends of the loculi. Herbert Anscomb (1892-1972) was Reeve of Oak Bay (1925-27), Mayor of Victoria (1929-31) and Co-Premier during the Coalition Government of the 1940's.

Additional map notes on Grant, the Men's Home, McBride and Giscombe.

George Lifton (left) and Alex Heard (right) of Stewart Monumental Works pose beside the empty double sepulchral sarcophagi for Anscomb in 1956.

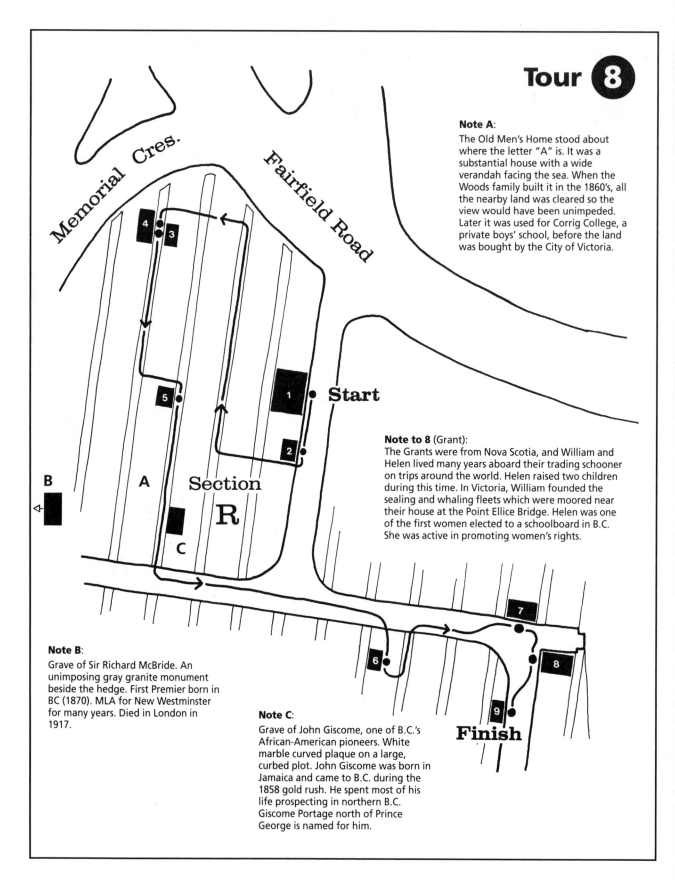

Tour 8

Note A:
The Old Men's Home stood about where the letter "A" is. It was a substantial house with a wide verandah facing the sea. When the Woods family built it in the 1860's, all the nearby land was cleared so the view would have been unimpeded. Later it was used for Corrig College, a private boys' school, before the land was bought by the City of Victoria.

Start

Note to 8 (Grant):
The Grants were from Nova Scotia, and William and Helen lived many years aboard their trading schooner on trips around the world. Helen raised two children during this time. In Victoria, William founded the sealing and whaling fleets which were moored near their house at the Point Ellice Bridge. Helen was one of the first women elected to a schoolboard in B.C. She was active in promoting women's rights.

Memorial Cres.

Fairfield Road

Section R

Finish

Note B:
Grave of Sir Richard McBride. An unimposing gray granite monument beside the hedge. First Premier born in BC (1870). MLA for New Westminster for many years. Died in London in 1917.

Note C:
Grave of John Giscome, one of B.C.'s African-American pioneers. White marble curved plaque on a large, curbed plot. John Giscome was born in Jamaica and came to B.C. during the 1858 gold rush. He spent most of his life prospecting in northern B.C. Giscome Portage north of Prince George is named for him.

The five tombstones that mark the graves of the Chungranes family.

The Romanesque style popular in late nineteenth century architecture has been used for the mausoleum of the Rithet family.

1. RUDLIN. Gray marble pedestal topped by a globe with an anchor carved in relief, by A. Stewart. George Rudlin (1835-1903) was a well-known captain for the Canadian Pacific Navigation Co., serving on the *S.S. Islander* and *S.S. Princess Victoria*.

2. MORTIMER. Gray granite pilaster topped by a Celtic cross. John Mortimer (1842-1921) was a monument maker. (See note on page 38).

3. HAY. White marble sculpted stump on a rusticated marble and granite base. The epitaph is chiselled on a scroll suspended from a branch. A.C. Hay (1858-1901) was a stonecutter.

4. WHITTINGTON. Rectangular raised bench made of maroon-coloured cement, with the name "Whittington" on a white marble plaque set into the side, and with a gray granite slant-faced marker on top. Graves of Percy R. Whittington (1876-1914) and family.

5. ROCKETT. (Proceed north from roadway immediately west of the Houston Mausoleum). Polished red granite column with a conical top supported by a 2-tiered circular base. It is likely the unmistakable rocket shape was intended as a representation of the unusual family name. Erected circa 1915 on the death of Margaret (1851-1915), wife of William Rockett (1848-1926), a carpenter.

6. SHAKESPEARE. Gray granite slant-faced slab, beside the hedge. Noah Shakespeare (1838-1921), a native of Brierly Hill, Staffordshire, was a former postmaster, mayor, and M.P. for Victoria, as well as an organizer of the anti-Oriental Workingman's Protective Association.

7. WILSON. Gray granite sepulchral sarcophagus with peaked top. Below it are the graves of Mary (1854-1917) and Keith (1847-1934) Wilson, a real estate broker whose palatial, turretted home, the "Parrot House" (now demolished) overlooked downtown Victoria. Their daughter, Victoria Jane (1878-1949), also buried here, made the house famous by raising birds there and leaving her fortune and the house to them, including Louis, a macaw, who stayed in the house for many years being cared for by a Chinese servant and receiving regular tots of brandy and walnuts.

8. SPENCER. Tall gray granite obelisk by A. Stewart, near Memorial Crescent, for David Spencer (1837-1920) and family. Spencer was the founder of David Spencer Ltd., department stores, later bought out by Eaton's.

Erection of Spencer's obelisk reflects the interest in Egypt spurred by the opening of King Tutankhamen's tomb in 1922. The Spencer mansion on Moss St. now is part of the Art Gallery.

9. LEWIS. A new marker for Lorne Lewis in the midst of an open, grassed area. Lewis, an African-American, was appointed police constable in gold rush Victoria by Gov. James Douglas, but because of his color, criminals objected to his authority. Later he served for many years as a special constable on the old Songhees Reserve.

This example of the stonecutter's art marks the grave of A.C. Hay, himself a stonecutter, although it is not known whether he made this tombstone. Several other sculpted stumps in Ross Bay Cemetery provide a diversion from the more traditional tablets, pedestals, and obelisks.

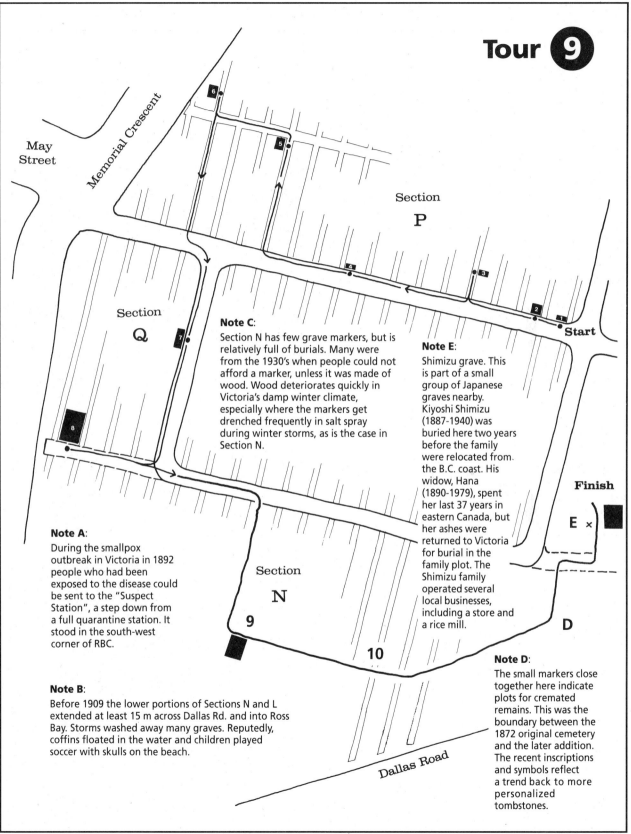

Tour 9

Section P

Start

Section Q

Note C:
Section N has few grave markers, but is relatively full of burials. Many were from the 1930's when people could not afford a marker, unless it was made of wood. Wood deteriorates quickly in Victoria's damp winter climate, especially where the markers get drenched frequently in salt spray during winter storms, as is the case in Section N.

Note E:
Shimizu grave. This is part of a small group of Japanese graves nearby. Kiyoshi Shimizu (1887-1940) was buried here two years before the family were relocated from the B.C. coast. His widow, Hana (1890-1979), spent her last 37 years in eastern Canada, but her ashes were returned to Victoria for burial in the family plot. The Shimizu family operated several local businesses, including a store and a rice mill.

Finish

E ×

11

Note A:
During the smallpox outbreak in Victoria in 1892 people who had been exposed to the disease could be sent to the "Suspect Station", a step down from a full quarantine station. It stood in the south-west corner of RBC.

Section N

9

10

D

Note D:
The small markers close together here indicate plots for cremated remains. This was the boundary between the 1872 original cemetery and the later addition. The recent inscriptions and symbols reflect a trend back to more personalized tombstones.

Note B:
Before 1909 the lower portions of Sections N and L extended at least 15 m across Dallas Rd. and into Ross Bay. Storms washed away many graves. Reputedly, coffins floated in the water and children played soccer with skulls on the beach.

Dallas Road

May Street

Memorial Crescent

Contemporary view looking north, with the mature trees and landscape architecture of historic Ross Bay Cemetery.

10. ASIAN GRAVES. A general grouping of tombstones in this area bear Japanese characters. After 1942 many of the Japanese graves were untended, and wooden post markers were not replaced. A monument to those whose graves are now unmarked is planned. After 1903 most Chinese were buried in the Chinese Cemetery at Harling Point. Burial records show one "Hindoo" buried in this area (now unmarked).

11. KOREYEDA. A gray granite screen to the memory of Taketomo Koreyeda, erected by "tenants and employees of the Pemberton Building in which he was accidentally killed on Oct. 8, 1912." He was caught in an elevator door and dragged to his death.

Additional map notes on smallpox, the RBC shoreline before 1909, wooden grave markers, cremation plots and Shimizu.

Chinese funerals featured roast pig and other foods which were left on the grave. Most Chinese graves were in Section L (to the east of N) before 1903, when the Chinese Cemetery was opened at Harling Point. Few Chinese burials took place after that at RBC.

Courtesy Provincial Archives of B.C., PABC No. 8469.

Section W is a small section, administered by the Anglican Church. It contains civilian graves, as well as several rows of post-World War I Canadian military graves under the auspices of the Commonwealth War Graves Commission.

1. AGNEW. Gray granite enclosure with white marble tablet set in a Romanesque arch. This unique grave was designed by Samuel Maclure, well-known Victoria architect. The Agnews had made a fortune in the silk trade in Montreal before moving to Victoria. Their home on Rockland Avenue became the Caroline Macklem Home for elderly women.

2. CROSS OF SACRIFICE. Tall gray granite cross on a wide octagonal base. Designed by Sir Reginald Blomfield after World War I. Examples are found throughout the British Commonwealth. It also serves as a memorial to those killed in World War II. There are about 150 military graves throughout RBC.

3. NAVAL MEMORIAL. Gray granite pedestal. It bears the names of Canadian men killed in action during World War I on HMCS *Galiano*, HMS *Victory*, HMS *Pembroke* and HM Submarine "H.10".

Additional map notes on James Anderson, World War I graves, Capt. Troup, the East Creek and Rev. Church.

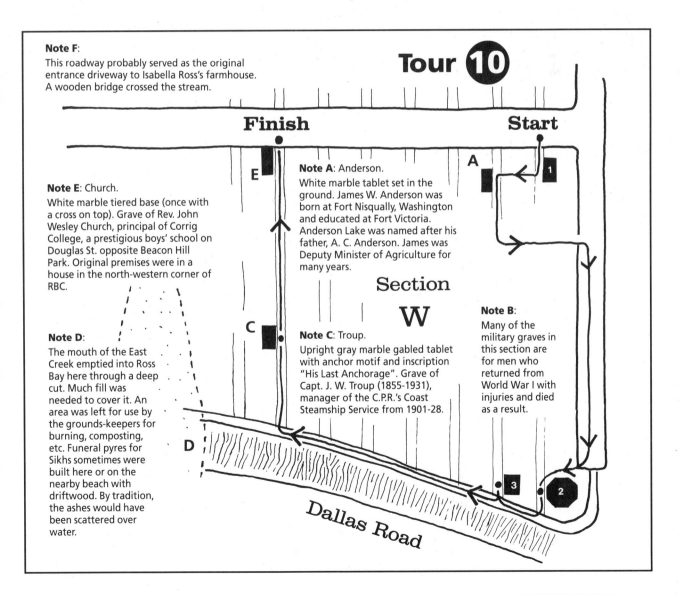

Tour ⑩

Note F: This roadway probably served as the original entrance driveway to Isabella Ross's farmhouse. A wooden bridge crossed the stream.

Finish

Start

E

A

1

Note E: Church. White marble tiered base (once with a cross on top). Grave of Rev. John Wesley Church, principal of Corrig College, a prestigious boys' school on Douglas St. opposite Beacon Hill Park. Original premises were in a house in the north-western corner of RBC.

Note A: Anderson. White marble tablet set in the ground. James W. Anderson was born at Fort Nisqually, Washington and educated at Fort Victoria. Anderson Lake was named after his father, A. C. Anderson. James was Deputy Minister of Agriculture for many years.

Section W

Note B: Many of the military graves in this section are for men who returned from World War I with injuries and died as a result.

C

Note C: Troup. Upright gray marble gabled tablet with anchor motif and inscription "His Last Anchorage". Grave of Capt. J. W. Troup (1855-1931), manager of the C.P.R.'s Coast Steamship Service from 1901-28.

Note D: The mouth of the East Creek emptied into Ross Bay here through a deep cut. Much fill was needed to cover it. An area was left for use by the grounds-keepers for burning, composting, etc. Funeral pyres for Sikhs sometimes were built here or on the nearby beach with driftwood. By tradition, the ashes would have been scattered over water.

D

3

2

Dallas Road

Section T was part of the cemetery expansion, with the first interment in 1907. The East Creek formed its western edge until filled in through the early 1920's. It is administered by the Anglican Church. Some wide pathways were divided into plots and sold in the 1980's.

1. WALBRAN. White marble, 2-tiered base only, probably once supporting a cross, by A. Stewart. Graves of Anne Mary Walbran (1848-1907), first person buried in Section T, and Captain John T. Walbran (1848-1913), master of the Canadian government steamship *Quadra* from 1891-1903. In 1909 he published *B.C. Coast Names*.

2.ꞁ FOSTER. Polished, red granite, truncated pedestal, by A. Stewart. Erected by subscription to athlete and trainer, Bob Foster (1847-1908). Note extensive laudatory epitaph.

3. POOLEY. White marble angel holding a rose and standing against rusticated cross. Grave of Charles Edward Pooley (1845-1912), M.L.A. for Esquimalt (1882-1906).

Pooley's angel likely was imported ready-made from a supplier. She has lost her right hand and rose to vandals and has been subject to paint-spray attacks. Local legend says she cries on nights with a full moon and smiles on the lovelorn.

The granite mausoleum of Harry D. Helmcken reflects the Egyptian-revival style popular in the early twentieth century. It is one of only ten mausolea at Ross Bay Cemetery.

4. CAMPBELL. Gray marble sculpted baby's chair with booties, bearing inscription "A little Hero". Grave of D.B. Campbell (died March 9th, 1913, aged 17 months).

5. HELMCKEN. Mausoleum in an Egyptian-inspired style made of gray granite. Contains loculi of Harry D. Helmcken (1859-1912) and family. Helmcken, a son of Dr. J.S. Helmcken, was a well-known lawyer and M.L.A. (1894-1903). He died in London while there for his health!

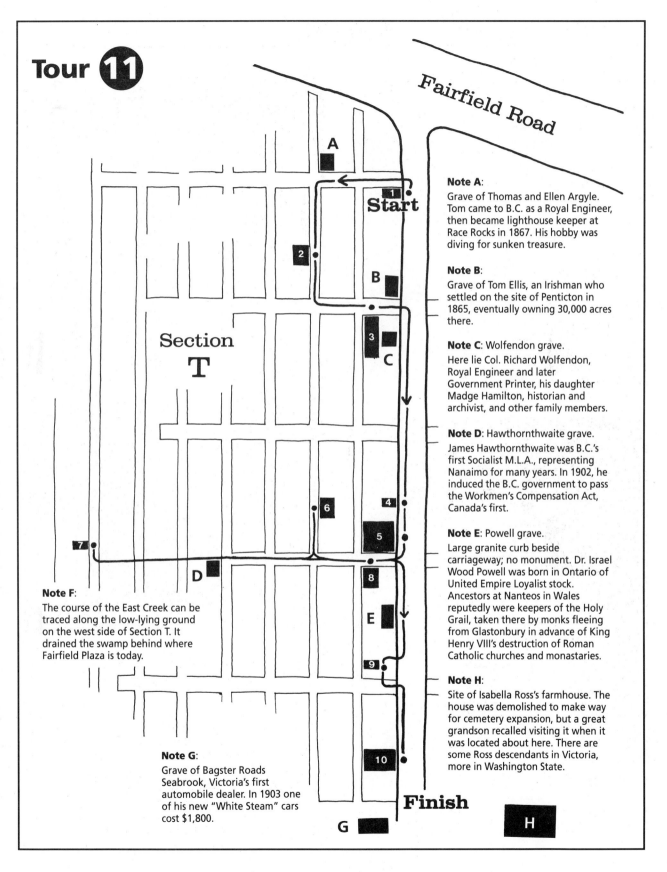

Tour ⑪

Fairfield Road

Start

A

B

C

D

E

Section T

Finish

G

H

Note A:
Grave of Thomas and Ellen Argyle. Tom came to B.C. as a Royal Engineer, then became lighthouse keeper at Race Rocks in 1867. His hobby was diving for sunken treasure.

Note B:
Grave of Tom Ellis, an Irishman who settled on the site of Penticton in 1865, eventually owning 30,000 acres there.

Note C: Wolfendon grave.
Here lie Col. Richard Wolfendon, Royal Engineer and later Government Printer, his daughter Madge Hamilton, historian and archivist, and other family members.

Note D: Hawthornthwaite grave.
James Hawthornthwaite was B.C.'s first Socialist M.L.A., representing Nanaimo for many years. In 1902, he induced the B.C. government to pass the Workmen's Compensation Act, Canada's first.

Note E: Powell grave.
Large granite curb beside carriageway; no monument. Dr. Israel Wood Powell was born in Ontario of United Empire Loyalist stock. Ancestors at Nanteos in Wales reputedly were keepers of the Holy Grail, taken there by monks fleeing from Glastonbury in advance of King Henry VIII's destruction of Roman Catholic churches and monastaries.

Note H:
Site of Isabella Ross's farmhouse. The house was demolished to make way for cemetery expansion, but a great grandson recalled visiting it when it was located about here. There are some Ross descendants in Victoria, more in Washington State.

Note F:
The course of the East Creek can be traced along the low-lying ground on the west side of Section T. It drained the swamp behind where Fairfield Plaza is today.

Note G:
Grave of Bagster Roads Seabrook, Victoria's first automobile dealer. In 1903 one of his new "White Steam" cars cost $1,800.

Photograph of Harry Helmcken (standing on right) with his brother, Dr. J. D. Helmcken (seated on left). The other man is unidentified. Private collection.

6. FENWICK. White marble Celtic cross for sisters Edith Mary and Isabel Fenwick, teachers at St. Margaret's School. Both drowned in the wreck of the S.S. *Iroquois* off Sidney, April 10, 1911. It was overloaded with hay.

7. MEDLEY. A bronze fire helmet mounted on a concrete pillow. This marker can be found easily by walking in a straight line west from the Helmcken mausoleum (No. 5). This unique tombstone honours Fred Medley (1891-1925), a Victoria fireman who was killed on duty when his speeding firetruck overturned on an icy street and pinned him underneath. The grave is on fill over the former East Creek. Note the manhole cover.

8. DEWDNEY. Gray granite Celtic cross. Grave of Hon. Edgar Dewdney (1835-1916), Lieutenant-Governor of B.C. (1892-97), and builder of the famed Dewdney Trail through southern B.C. in the 1860's.

9. GREAVES. (Pronounced Graves). Rough-hewn gray granite Celtic cross. Grave of Joseph Blackburn Greaves (1831-1915), one of the founders of the Douglas Lake Cattle Co., in 1884. The Douglas Lake Ranch later became Canada's largest privately owned ranch.

10. JOHNSON. Mausoleum constructed of rough-hewn gray granite blocks. Contains remains of Byron Ingemar ("Boss") Johnson (1890-1964), Liberal Premier of B.C., from 1947-52 who introduced compulsory hospital insurance to the province. Johnson was of Icelandic descent and was raised in the Fernwood neighborhood where there was a large Icelandic community. He operated a trucking business.

Additional map notes on Argyle, Ellis, Wolfendon, Hawthornthwaite, Powell, the East Creek, Seabrook and Ross.

The unique fire helmet grave marker for Fred Medley reminds the viewer of this city fireman's tragic death while on duty in 1925.

Tour 12

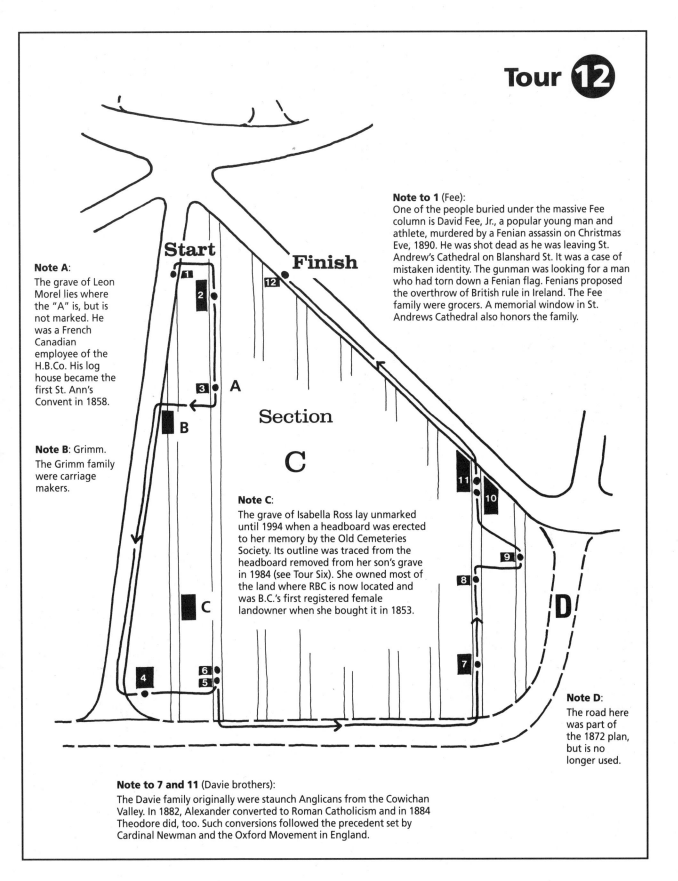

Start

Finish

Note A:
The grave of Leon Morel lies where the "A" is, but is not marked. He was a French Canadian employee of the H.B.Co. His log house became the first St. Ann's Convent in 1858.

Note B: Grimm. The Grimm family were carriage makers.

Note to 1 (Fee):
One of the people buried under the massive Fee column is David Fee, Jr., a popular young man and athlete, murdered by a Fenian assassin on Christmas Eve, 1890. He was shot dead as he was leaving St. Andrew's Cathedral on Blanshard St. It was a case of mistaken identity. The gunman was looking for a man who had torn down a Fenian flag. Fenians proposed the overthrow of British rule in Ireland. The Fee family were grocers. A memorial window in St. Andrews Cathedral also honors the family.

Section C

Note C:
The grave of Isabella Ross lay unmarked until 1994 when a headboard was erected to her memory by the Old Cemeteries Society. Its outline was traced from the headboard removed from her son's grave in 1984 (see Tour Six). She owned most of the land where RBC is now located and was B.C.'s first registered female landowner when she bought it in 1853.

Note D:
The road here was part of the 1872 plan, but is no longer used.

Note to 7 and 11 (Davie brothers):
The Davie family originally were staunch Anglicans from the Cowichan Valley. In 1882, Alexander converted to Roman Catholicism and in 1884 Theodore did, too. Such conversions followed the precedent set by Cardinal Newman and the Oxford Movement in England.

Section C in the original plan for RBC of 1873 was reserved for the use of the Roman Catholic Church, which still retains control over burials in it. Of special interest is the cosmopolitan mix of people buried here which include: native Indians, Irish, Scottish, English, Dutch, Germans, French, Americans, Syrians and Canadians.

1. FEE. Tall, polished red granite column, topped by an urn, and supported by a substantial pedestal. Grave of D.F. Fee (1827-1900), a grocer on North Park Street.

2. SEHL. Polished red granite column with urn to Frank Sehl (1831-90) and family. Sehl was proprietor of the Teutonia Saloon on Government St. Note also the white marble scroll-faced tombstone with a rosebud motif on the back. It marks the graves of two Sehl children.

3. SEHL. Polished red granite screen. Graves of Jacob Sehl (1831-90) and family. J. Sehl operated a furniture factory.

4. LARBONNE. White marble ledger-stone with cross on top. The epitaph for Marie Larbonne (1819-92) is interesting, if not entirely devoid of anglicisms in the French and Latin texts: "ICI REPOSE MARIE LARBONNE NEE A NABIS DEPARTEMENS [sic] DES BASSES PYRENNEES FRANCE. DECEDEE A VICTORIA LE 5th [sic] OCTOBER [sic] 1892 A LAGE [sic] DE 73 ANS. REQUESCAT [sic] IN PEACE [sic]".

Here Lies
Isabella Mainville
ROSS

Born Jan 10, 1808
Died in Victoria
April 23, 1885

She came here in 1843 with her husband, Chief Trader Charles Ross, who was in charge of building Fort Victoria. After his death she bought the land upon which you are standing for a farm. By so doing she became the first woman to own land in what is now British Columbia.

Erected by the
Old Cemeteries Society, 1994

5. BAHASH. Upright, white marble tablet with cross, by Wasto & Robertson. Grave of Joseph Bahash (1872-96), a Syrian. Note Arabic epitaph.

6. RAHY. White marble tablet with cross and crown motif. The Rahy brothers operated the Syrian Store on Douglas St., dealing in dry goods and jewelry from the Middle East.

7. DAVIE. White marble cross with lamb motif, over a coat of arms, by G. Rudge. Graves of Alexander Edmund Batson Davie (1848-89) and family. Davie, a former Cariboo lawyer, was Premier of B.C. from 1887 until his death.

8. MADDEN. Gray granite peaked ledger-stone. Grave of Sierra Nevada Madden (1855-85). Born during a raging storm in the Sierra Nevada mountains while her parents were crossing in a covered wagon to the California goldfields. Came to B.C. with her parents, but eloped with Madden.

9. REALIS. Upright sandstone Gothic-style, gabled tablet. Grave of Antonio Realis (1807-79), of Italy.

10. McQUADE. Gray marble pedestal with arched cornice, topped by a cross, by G. Rudge. Graves of Peter McQuade (1823-84) and family. He founded well-known ship chandlery firm.

11. DAVIE. Plot surrounded by a gray granite curb, but contains no monument, except for a recent granite plaque commemorating Hon. Theodore Davie (1825-98), Premier of B.C. from 1892-95 and Chief Justice of B.C. from 1895-98. The Parliament Buildings were started during his term as Premier.

12. VIGELIUS. Polished red granite column, topped by a cross, by A. Stewart. Note white marble grave cover with inset carved floral garland. Grave of Louis Vigelius (1838-1900), a city alderman in 1886 and co-proprietor of the St. Nicholas Baths and Hair Dressing Saloon on Government Street.

Additional map notes on Fee, Davie, Morel, Grimm, Ross and 1872 road.

The new headboard for Isabella Ross copies the shape of the one that stood on her son's grave until 1984. Hundreds of wooden markers once were found at Ross Bay Cemetery. They were painted white to simulate marble, but over many years the paint wore off, leaving a rough, textured surface.

These sections formed part of Isabella Ross's Fowl Bay Farm (as spelled in the records) and her farmhouse stood in the lower part of what is now Section V. The property passed out of the Ross family in 1876 and went through numerous owners until the City of Victoria acquired it for cemetery expansion. The Roman Catholic Church manages these sections.

1. BURKE. Upright white and gray marble pedestal topped by a ball with an engraved cross, by A. Stewart. In memory of Patrick D.M. Burke (1865-1901), who "perished in the wreck of the S.S. Islander near Juneau in one of his brave acts on August 15th, 1901". He was listed in the city directory as proprietor of the Bee-Hive Saloon on Fort Street.

2. WILKES. Upright white marble cross and tablet, draped and garlanded. Grave of Harriet Ann Wilkes (1879-1920) and her one day old daughter. Note the oval lead frame inset into the cross to hold a photograph. This is the only extant example in RBC of this once-popular custom.

3. CASHMAN. Recent polished gray granite plaque laid flat on the ground. Grave of Nellie Cashman (1844-1925). It reads: "Friend of the sick and the hungry and to all men. Heroic apostolate of service among the western and northern frontier miners. Miner's Angel, 1872-1924 in Nevada, in Arizona, in California, in the Cassiar, in the Yukon, in Alaska. Born in Ireland. Died with the Sisters of Saint Ann at St. Joseph's Hospital, Victoria, B.C. January 4, 1925. Requiescat in Pace".

4. SISTERS OF ST. ANN. This is a large plot dominated by white marble crosses on tablets marking the graves of the Sisters. In the center of the plot is a white marble pedestal topped with a cross, by A. Stewart. It commemorates the Sisters who had died from 1864-1908, prior to the use of this burial place. (They had been buried in the grounds of St. Ann's Academy). The Sisters had originally come to Victoria from Quebec in 1858 and are noted for their early and continuing role in education and health care.

5. BRABANT. White marble 2-tiered base (probably once supporting a cross). Grave of Rev. Augustus Joseph Brabant (1845-1912). Born in Belgium, he had come to B.C. in 1869 and in 1874 established a mission at Hesquiat on the west coast of Vancouver Island where he remained for 34 years.

6. SISTERS OF ST. CLARE. White marble statue of St. Clare, supported on a pedestal. Inscription reads: "My Beloved Daughters (Saint Clare). Gift of Margaret J. Murphy of New York". The Sisters, known generally as "the Poor Clares", are a cloistered order. Their convent stood for many years in Oak Bay, but has now moved to Duncan. St. Clare is the patron saint of television, based on a TV-like vision she had on her cell wall.

7. PICCA. Upright, cast concrete tablet with a mosaic tiled front and topped by a cross. Grave of Ferucio Della Picca (1895-1913).

8. PETER. Gray marble pedestal with bevelled top, supporting a cross. Graves of Catherine Gabriel (1884-1909) and Chief Aleck Peters (1876-1943).

9. SIOMAX. The plot contains 2 upright monuments. The northernmost is a white marble tablet topped by a cross and bearing the entwined IHS motif. Grave of James Siomax (1797-1892) "Chief of Songhees Tribe". The southernmost marker is a white marble tablet with a cross and crown motif, by A. Stewart. Grave of Mary (1836-1904), wife of "Chief Jim".

10. GUNION. The plot contains 3 markers. Note the southernmost, a low sandstone obelisk with an inset motif of a cross draped with a fuschia. It is in memory of Nicholas Khanishten "a chief of the Songish nation" (died December 21st, 1888, aged 100 years). The middle monument is an upright white marble tablet with an inset motif of a cross draped with morning glory. It is in memory of Mary Ann (1847-88), wife of C. Montobio.

This photograph was taken in 1982 and shows the white marble crosses in the plot for the Sisters of St. Ann. Repeated vandalism in the mid-1980's and the high cost of repairs convinced the Church to replace the crosses with sturdier granite plaques. Only a few crosses remain near the hedge at the eastern side of the large plot. The sisters buried on the St. Ann's Academy grounds before 1908 were exhumed in the 1970's and re-buried here.

Additional map notes on Picca, Springett, Sister Mary Osithe, Rosso and Native graves.

Tour 13

Start

Section U

Section V

Finish

Fairfield Road

LANE

Plot For Sisters of St. Ann

Note A:
Grave of Louis Springett. Marked by a large, white shell. Springett, an Englishman, moved with his family to Maple Bay where they operated a guest house. Louis preferred fishing and painting to helping run the business. The shell was brought by one of his daughters from a sailing trip to the south Pacific, a fitting tribute to one who loved the sea so much.

Note to 7 (Picca):
Fred Picca (a shorter version of Ferucio Della Picca) was only 18 when he drowned in the Gorge while swimming with his younger brothers in the summer of 1913. His father was a marble worker and probably made the distinctive mosaic tablet himself.

Note B:
Sister Mary Osithe was the art teacher at St. Ann's from 1897 to 1941. She taught many girls in crayons, oils, water color and china painting. Many of her own fine oil paintings are displayed in the restored St. Ann's Academy.

Note C: Rosso Mausoleum.
An addition to RBC in the 1990's was the Rosso family's mausoleum, constructed by Mortimer's Monumental Works. In their native Italy such mausoleums were much more common than here, although the trend to build them is on the increase. Gelsino Giuseppe "Joe" Rosso (1911-1998) ran the Figaro Barber Shop for many years.

Note to 8, 9, 10:
Why do these tombstones have dates of death that pre-date the opening of this section by many years? These graves of First Nations people were once in the Roman Catholic cemetery on the old Songhees Reserve, but were moved here in 1912 when the Songhees moved to their new reserve in Esquimalt.

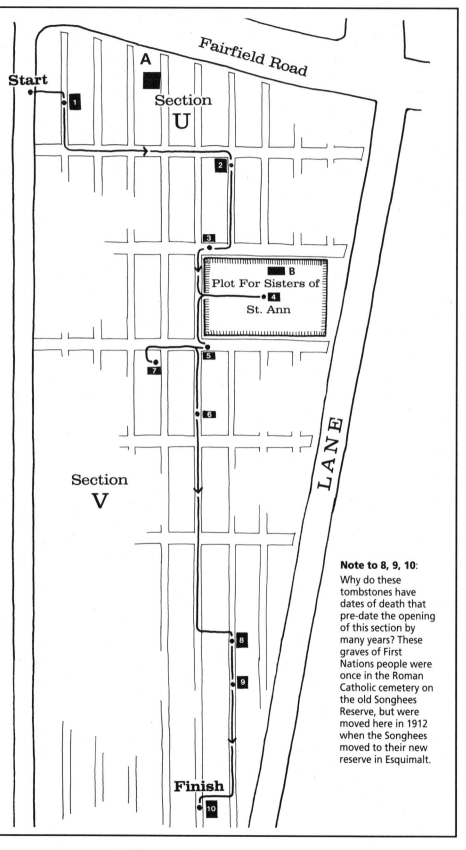

C

Notes on Monument Makers

A large proportion of the tombstones located in Ross Bay Cemetery bear the maker's name, usually on the bottom, right hand corner. The majority of signed stones were produced or at least inscribed by Victoria stone cutters and comparisons of styles indicate the majority of unsigned ones were made by the same local makers. While many makers' names appear, a few predominate: Bell, Bradbury, Fisher, Foster, Kirsop, Mortimer, Phillips, Rudge and Stewart. In the brief biographical notes below these men have been given more emphasis, but all known makers whose work was examined in Ross Bay Cemetery are included.

Some completed monuments were brought from other centers as near as Nanaimo, or as far away as Ontario, San Francisco, and England.

Mary Philpot in her M.A. thesis, *In This Neglected Spot: The Rural Cemetery Landscape in Southern British Columbia,* notes that by the turn of the twentieth century monument makers frequently used mass-produced dies onto which they only had to add epitaphs and occasionally carved motifs. The repetition of motifs points to the fact that monument makers during the nineteenth century were also probably using pattern guides.

Philpot also notes that the materials used by Victoria monument makers often came from afar. Sandstone (used only until about 1885 and mainly by Foster in RBC) came from Haddington Island. White marble came from Vermont, Italy, Sweden or Scotland; blue or grey marble came from Vermont. Gray granite frequently was obtained in B.C. from Nelson Island, Texada Island or Granite Island. Red Granite came from Aberdeen (Scotland), Sweden and New Brunswick.

Four architects are known to have designed monuments at RBC. Samuel Maclure, Francis Mawson Rattenbury and Thomas Sorby were British Columbia architects who each have at least one piece at RBC. Sir Reginald Blomfield of England designed the Cross of Sacrifice.

Non-Victoria Makers

Maker	Location	Date of Earliest Work in RBC
Canadian Granite Co.	Ottawa, Ontario	1889
Carrara Marble Works	Plymouth, England	1881
Copas, W.	Swansea, Wales	1900
Cullett and Sons	Toronto, Ontario	1903
Daniel, J.	San Francisco	1874
Henderson, Alex	Nanaimo, B.C.	1904
Robertson, T. S.	unknown	1892
Sanders	London, England	1876
Venn, Moses	Metlakahtla, B.C.	1879
White Bronze Co.	St. Thomas, Ontario	1888

A large number of cast tombstones, mainly obelisks, are located in RBC, and probably most came from the White Bronze Co., though only one bears the foundry's name.

Some of the fine statuary at RBC was produced in Victoria. George Kirsop's work, for example, can be seen on the Deans statue symbolizing faith and the girl on the Woods grave. Other statues, such as the Pooley angel, likely came ready-made from Carrara, Italy or other marble works.

Victoria Makers

BELL, WILLIAM. Usually signed himself "Bell". At least one tombstone in RBC by Bell dates from 1882, the first year he is listed in the Victoria directory as a stonecutter, with residence at the corner of Broad and View Streets. By 1889 his address was 84 Dallas Road. There are no further references to him in the directories after 1891.

BRADBURY, THOMAS WILKINSON (1862-1957). Usually signed himself "T. Bradbury". Born in St. Helen's, Lancashire, Bradbury moved to Victoria in 1887. Here he entered into the construction business, including stone-cutting and monument making. His offices and yard were listed at the corner of Cormorant and Blanshard Streets in 1896, and he was reported in the *Colonist* as being the agent for the Vancouver Granite Quarries and an importer of Scottish and other granites. During the construction of the Parliament Buildings he was construction director. He also worked on the Nanaimo Courthouse. In 1901 he moved to California where he helped in the rebuilding of Stanford University after the 1906 earthquake. Returning to Victoria in 1927 he again became a contractor and monument dealer.

FISHER, JAMES. Usually signed himself "J. Fisher". He operated the Albion Granite and Marble Works in Victoria from approximately 1884-91. An advertisement in the *Colonist* stated: "All work guaranteed equal to any on the Pacific Coast and at reasonable rates".

FOSTER, ROBERT (1831-80). Usually signed himself "Foster" in cursive script. A native of Yorkshire, Foster began making monuments in Victoria sometime before 1866 when he was commissioned by the men of *H.M.S. Sutlej* to make a memorial to their fellow shipmates who had died since being at the Esquimalt Station. (This weathered monument still stands in Pioneer Square). He was described in the directories of the 1860's and 70's as being a stonecutter and builder, with his address variously as at the Rock Bay Bridge or Point Ellice.

GILARDI, M. Usually signed himself "M. Gilardi". A native of Lombardy, Italy, Gilardi (variously spelled Gilardia in the directories) has only two known signed works in RBC, although he likely made others. In 1890 he was listed in the directory as a marble cutter, with residence at 135 Vancouver Street.

KIRSOP, GEORGE (1825-97). Usually signed himself "G. Kirsop". Born in Newcastle-on-Tyne, Kirsop began making monuments and cutting stone in Victoria in about 1875. His business address was on Chatham Street. He was a member of the Reformed Episcopal Church.

McRAE. This name was found once as "McRae and Wasto" on a tombstone of 1893.

MORTIMER, JOHN (1842-1921). Usually signed himself "J. Mortimer". He started in business in Victoria in 1877 and his early business card listed his stoneyard on Government Street near the James Bay Bridge. He dealt in marble, free stone (sandstone), granite and also plaster decorations. He was later joined in business by his son Arthur. The successor company of Mortimer's Monumental Works still operates in Victoria.

PHILLIPS, JOSEPH EVA (1850-1908). Usually signed himself as "J.E. Phillips", but occasionally as "J.E.P." Born in Cornwall, England and apprenticed there as a stonemason, Phillips arrived in Victoria in 1881. By 1887 he was listed in the directory as an "Importer and Dealer in all kinds of Polished Granite and Marble". The *Colonist* in 1896 mentioned that he was a "dealer in granite and marble monuments, cut stone, etc." with offices and yards at 74-76 View Street and at Ross Bay Cemetery. During the 1890's he was a Victoria City alderman.

ROBERTSON, ALEX. This name was found twice, both times as "Wasto and Robertson" on tombstones made in 1896. The directory of 1890 lists Alex Robertson as a stonecutter with rooms at the Windsor Hotel (Government Street).

RUDGE, GEORGE (1854-1934). Usually signed himself as "G. Rudge", although from approximately 1878-1891 in combination as "Wright and Rudge". Rudge was born in St. Stephens, New Brunswick, the son of a marble dealer, with whom he apprenticed. He arrived in Victoria in 1875 after having plied the marble business in San Francisco and Seattle. In 1891 he moved to Port Simpson, B.C., where he continued making monuments and is noted for his totemic images in stone to be found in native Indian cemeteries on the Queen Charlotte Islands, Port Simpson, Port Essington, Kitamaat, and Hazelton. He moved back to Victoria in 1917 to retire and lived on Thurlow Street, close to Ross Bay Cemetery. Rudge is also noted for having secured the contract to quarry granite for the Parliament Buildings and for his carvings at Craigdarroch Castle. A number of his sons also became stonecutters in Victoria.

STEWART, ALEXANDER (1864-1943). Usually signed himself "A. Stewart". He began monument making in Victoria in 1886 and continued until just prior to his death. His first office was located on Yates Street, but in 1911 moved to the corner of May and Eberts Streets near RBC, where the Stewart Monumental Works still operates.

WASTO, M. Signed himself variously as "M. Wasto" or in conjunction with others (see *McRae* and *Robertson*). In partnership with F.T. Mossford (whose signature does not appear on any tombstones in RBC), Wasto operated the Victoria Granite and Marble Works on Fort Street during the mid 1890's.

WRIGHT, HUGH, M. Wright's signature never appears alone on a tombstone in RBC, but from 1878-81 in conjunction as "Wright and Rudge".

The stone yard of Mortimer's Monumental Works in the early years of the twentieth century. Owner and founder, John Mortimer, stands center left wearing a jacket and bowler hat, surrounded by stonecutters wearing traditional aprons. This yard was located on the 700 block of Courtney Street and was the second yard of this firm in Victoria. Its first had been on Government Street near the old James Bay Bridge. Photograph courtesy Mortimer's Monumental Works (1977) Ltd.

Key to Tombstone Symbols at Ross Bay Cemetery

The vast majority of tombstones at Ross Bay Cemetery bear symbols popular in the last quarter of the nineteenth century and first quarter of the twentieth. Most interments were of Christians, so crosses of all types are the most common symbols. Following are some of the others most frequently found and their meanings.

Clasped Hands
friendship; the last good-bye; also the secret Masonic handshake (the Masons or Freemasons are a fraternal organization)

Urn
classical representation of death; also the eternal dwelling or house

Rose
love; regeneration; also Christ's wounds

Open Book
the Bible

All-Seeing Eye
Masonic symbol representing the Great Architect of the Universe (included in US $1 bill)

Oak Leaves
strength (moral as well as physical)

Weeping Willow
mourning; also everlasting life

Torch or Lamp
God and light; also the eternal spirit and cleansing by fire

Broken Rose Bud
almost always on a child's grave to indicate life cut short

Fleur-de-lis
the Trinity; also the three Christian virtues: faith, hope and charity

Chain
the bonds between Heaven and Earth; also Odd Fellows (a fraternal organization)

IHS
Latin *Iesus hominum salvator* (Jesus, saviour of man); or Greek abbreviation of IHCOYC (Jesus)

Anchor
Christian faith; often associated with naval burials

Lily
purity, innocence, virginity; also surrender to the will of God

Passion Flower
the passion and death of Christ; redemption; crucifixion

Shamrock
the Trinity; also connection to Ireland

Acorn
plenty, prosperity, fruitfulness; also the power of the spirit

Square and Calipers
stone mason's tools, found only on Mason's graves

The trend after World War I was for simple headstones with minimal inscriptions and symbols. In the 1980's, the trend began toward more individuality in headstones, encouraged by computerized sandblasting technology. At Ross Bay Cemetery, look at the most recent stones, often found in the areas reserved for cremations, for some unique inscriptions and symbols.

Key to Styles of Monuments

Scroll-faced marker

Shouldered tablet   Simple tablet

Screen

Slant-faced marker

Plaque

Raised bench

Ledger-stone with cross

Classical column

Truncated obelisk

Monument in the style of
the Albert Memorial, London

Celtic cross

Bi-columnar monument

Gabled Gothic tablet

Broken column

Double sepulchral sarcophagus

Pilaster

Pedestal

Column topped
by draped urn

Mausoleum
(not to scale)

Obelisk

Screen topped by pilasters
supporting a pediment

Index

Acknowledgements

In 1982 when I was writing the first edition of the *Historic Guide to Ross Bay Cemetery* I was assisted and encouraged by many people, including: Greg Evans, Linda Eversole, Richard Collier, Douglas Franklin, Alex Heard, Ainslie Helmcken, Catherine Henderson, Rob Lifton, Ken and Gail Mann, Ken Pedlow, Ian Phillips, Charles Ross, Bert Santarossa, Martin Segger, Warren F. Sommer, Stuart Stark, Anne Thompson and Ron Walker.

Since then the number of people who have assisted me in gaining a better understanding of the history of Ross Bay Cemetery is in the thousands. As a direct result of the first edition I became involved in the formation of the Old Cemeteries Society and have been privileged to have been a part of its very active year-round walking tour program since it began in 1987. Much insight has come from people taking the tours. Much has come from colleagues in the Old Cemeteries Society and others who research diverse aspects of local and cemetery history. I hesitate to single out any individuals for fear of omitting someone, but I am grateful for help from the following for information specifically used in the revised edition: Kathryn Bridge, Rosemary Crawford, Sheila Daly, Sherry Edmunds Flett, Michael Halleran, Chris Hanna, Fred Hook, Bonita Jackson, Mary Doody Jones, Grant Keddie, Dennis Minaker, Brad Morrison, Carey Pallister, Glenn Perlstrom, Charlene Rees, Terry Reksten, Kiyoshi Shimizu, Yvonne Van Ruskenveld and Janice Wesolowski.

Special thanks to Martin Segger, Douglas Franklin and Heritage Architectural Guides for publishing the *Historic Guide to Ross Bay Cemetery* in 1983, and to Diane Morriss and Sono Nis Press for publishing the revised edition. I am grateful to Yvonne Van Ruskenveld for her editing.

What started out as a short-term project at Ross Bay Cemetery has extended to almost two decades. Throughout this time my wife, Donna, has continued to encourage and help me in my research and cemetery projects. I would like to give special thanks to her and our two grown children, Chris and Kate, for enduring with great humour what some consider an unusual hobby.